American
English in Mind

Herbert Puchta & Jeff Stranks

Workbook 1

CAMBRIDGE
UNIVERSITY PRESS

CAMBRIDGE
UNIVERSITY PRESS

32 Avenue of the Americas, New York, NY 10013-2473, USA

Cambridge University Press is part of the University of Cambridge.

It furthers the University's mission by disseminating knowledge in the pursuit of education, learning and research at the highest international levels of excellence.

www.cambridge.org
Information on this title: www.cambridge.org/9780521733397

First published 2011
11th printing 2015

Printed and bound in Italy by Rotolito Lombarda SpA

A catalog record for this publication is available from the British Library.

ISBN 978-0-521-73333-5 Student's Book 1
ISBN 978-0-521-73334-2 Combo 1A
ISBN 978-0-521-73335-9 Combo 1B
ISBN 978-0-521-73339-7 Workbook 1
ISBN 978-0-521-73340-3 Teacher's Edition 1
ISBN 978-0-521-73341-0 Class Audio 1
ISBN 978-0-521-73327-4 Classware 1
ISBN 978-0-521-73342-7 Testmaker 1
ISBN 978-0-521-73364-9 DVD 1

Art direction, book design and layout: Pentacor plc
Photo research: Pronk and Associates

Contents

1 Welcome

1 Remember and check

Match the parts of the sentences. Then check with the text on page 2 of the Student's Book.

...c...	1	Jack is	a	from Canada.
....	2	Monica is	b	from Guatemala.
....	3	Carlos is	c	from the United States.
....	4	Ken and Barbara are	d	from Italy.

2 Grammar

✱ The verb *be*

a Look at the information about the summer camp participants. Write sentences.

Name	Country	Age	Student	Room
Marco	Colombia	19	✗	101
Lien	China	16	✓	116
Darius	The United States	17	✓	209
Priya and Sita	India	18	✗	112
Patrick and Alan	Canada	16	✓	205

1 Marco *Marco is from Colombia. He's 19. He isn't a student.*
   He's in Room 101.

2 Lien ....

   ....

3 Darius ....

   ....

4 Priya and Sita ....

   ....

5 Patrick and Alan ....

   ....

✱ Possessive adjectives

b Complete the table with possessive adjectives.

I	you	he	she
my	....	....	....
it	we	you	they
its	....	....	....

c <u>Underline</u> the correct words.

1 *I / My* live in Canada.
   I / My name's Pauline.

2 *I / My* brother Andy has a pet mouse. *He / His* keeps it in *he / his* room.

3 *I / My* sister has a poster of Coldplay in *she / her* bedroom.

4 Tell me about *you / your* friends.

5 *We / Our* don't have a dog. *We / Our* parents don't like animals.

6 Uncle Joe and Aunt Sophie live in Australia. *They / Their* house is great! *They / Their* want us to visit them next year.

✳ The verb *have*

d Look at the table and write sentences. Use the correct form of *have*.

	Jordan	Helen
green eyes	✗	✓
a big family	✗	✓
a bicycle	✓	✗
a dog	✗	✗
black hair	✓	✓
a lot of DVDs	✓	✗
a little brother	✗	✓
a big bedroom	✗	✓

1 Jordan / green eyes

Jordan doesn't have green eyes.

2 Helen / a little brother

....

3 Helen / a lot of DVDs

....

4 Jordan / a bicycle

....

5 Jordan and Helen / black hair

....

6 Helen / a big bedroom

....

7 Jordan / a big family

....

8 Jordan and Helen / a dog

....

✳ *There is / there are* and prepositions of place

e Complete the sentences with *there is* or *there are*. Then ⟨circle⟩ the items in the picture that are different from the sentences.

1 *There is* a sofa in the living room.

2 .... a table next to the sofa.

3 .... two books on the table.

4 .... a bag under the table.

5 .... three pens in the bag.

6 .... two lamps behind the sofa.

7 .... two dogs on the sofa.

8 .... is a cat between the dogs.

f Underline the prepositions of place in Exercise 1e.

3 Vocabulary

✱ Colors

a Find the 10 colors in the wordsnake and (circle) them.

blueredgreenwhitebrownpinkblackyelloworangegray

b Answer the questions with your own information.

1 What color is your desk? ....

2 What color are the walls in your room? ....

3 What color is your bag? ....

4 What color is your phone? ....

5 What is your favorite color? ....

✱ Rooms and furniture

c (Circle) 14 things you can find in rooms in a house (→ ← ↓ or ↑).

B	A	T	B	E	D	T	O
T	A	B	L	E	C	E	G
B	S	T	O	V	E	L	U
A	M	S	C	H	A	I	R
T	F	W	F	O	I	O	C
H	R	O	O	D	R	T	A
T	I	D	K	N	I	S	B
U	D	N	E	T	U	O	I
B	G	I	R	R	O	F	N
R	E	W	O	H	S	A	E
S	L	T	R	O	U	M	T

d Write the names of the rooms.

1 This room usually has a sofa, chairs and a TV.

living room

2 This room usually has a fridge, a stove and a sink.

....

3 This room usually has a table and chairs.

....

4 This room usually has a bathtub, a shower or both.

....

5 This room usually has a bed and sometimes a desk and a chair.

....

4 Pronunciation

✱ /h/ (have)

a ▶ CD3 T09 (Circle) the words that start with *h*. Then listen and repeat.

1 Hi, my name is Helena.

2 How are you?

3 Henry has a big house.

4 Do you live here?

5 How many brothers do you have?

b ▶ CD3 T10 Complete the dialogue with the words from Exercise 4a. You will use some words more than once. Then listen, check and repeat.

Helena: [1] _Hi_ , [2] ....

Henry: Hi, [3] .... [4] .... are you?

Helena: I'm fine. Do you live [5] .... ?

Henry: No, that's Joe's [6] ....

Helena: Wow! He has a big [7] .... !

Henry: I know. He [8] .... eight brothers and sisters.

Helena: Really? [9] .... many brothers and sisters do you [10] .... ?

Henry: I [11] .... one sister. We have a small [12] ....

5 Culture in mind

  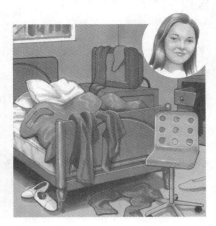

Correct the information. Then check with the text on page 6 of the Student's Book.

1   Vera has a small room.

Vera has a big room.

2   Vera has a green rug in her bedroom.

3   Vera and Trish have posters in their rooms.

4   Kwan shares a room with his sisters.

5   There is one bed in Kwan's room.

6   Trish's room is very clean.

7   Trish's favorite thing in her room is her black desk.

8   There are clothes on Trish's computer.

6 Study help

✱ Vocabulary

Words in a dictionary are in alphabetical order. Sometimes vocabulary lists in books are in alphabetical order, too. For example, irregular verbs are listed in the back of your Student's Book on page 122 in alphabetical order. Using alphabetical order helps you find words easily. You might want to organize vocabulary words in your notebook in alphabetical order.

a Put these words in the correct place in the list.

> toilet   chair   bathtub   shower   sink

bathtub ....

bed   sofa

cabinet   table

....

door   window

....

b Now put these words in alphabetical order.

> blue   green   red   gray   black
> brown   pink   orange   white   yellow

....

....

....

....

....

7 Read

a Read the title and look at the pictures. Where does the family live?

The Sleepers Sleep in a Cave!

The Sleeper family lives in a cave. Curtis Sleeper, Deborah Sleeper and their three children live in a house inside a cave in Missouri in the United States. Their house is very big. It has many things that most houses have – bedrooms, a kitchen, a living room and a lot of furniture. It even has large windows and a front door. However, the walls of the rooms are part of the cave, so the rooms inside the house look unusual. Many of the rooms inside the house are unusual.

The Sleeper's house is cool in the summer and warm in the winter. It is also very quiet, except when Curtis and Deborah's son is playing music!

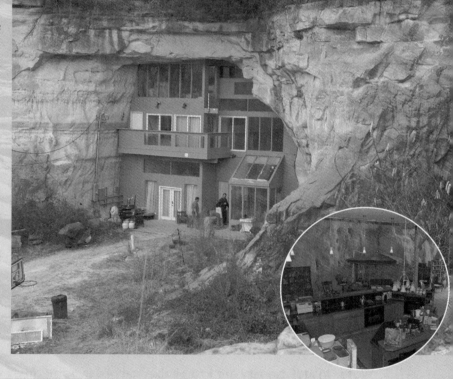

b Read the text and answer the questions.

1 Where is the house? *In a cave in Missouri.*

2 How many people live in the house? _____

3 What are some rooms the house has? _____

4 Who plays music? _____

8 Write

Write an email to one of the children in the Sleeper family. Include this information:

Paragraph 1

- Ask questions about the cave house.

Paragraph 2

- Tell the child about your house.

WRITING TIP

Before you write

- Read the directions carefully. Are you sure you know what you have to do? What do you have to write about? How much do you have to write?

- Think about what you are going to write. Are there any words you don't know in English?

- Tell a partner what you are going to write about. Does he/she understand your ideas? Ask each other questions about your plans and help each other with any words you don't know.

Unit check

1 Fill in the blanks

Complete the text with words in the box.

| have | is | blue | ~~Mexican~~ | my | the United States | has | his | our | windows |

Hi, I'm Eva. I'm from Mexico. My mother is ___Mexican___ , but my father [1]_____ American. I
[2]_____ a sister and a brother. I share a room with [3]_____ sister. Our room is very big. It
[4]_____ two beds. It only has one desk, so we study at different times. My brother has [5]_____
own room, but it's small. [6]_____ house is big. It's [7]_____ , and it has a lot of [8]_____ .
Every summer, we visit my grandparents in [9]_____ . They have a nice apartment in San Diego.

| 9 |

2 Choose the correct answers

Circle the correct answer: a, b or c.

1 Raul _____ from Italy.
  a be   b (is)   c are

2 Mr. Lee is _____ .
  a South Korean   b South Korea   c South Koreas

3 There _____ two computers in my house.
  a be   b is   c are

4 There's a chair _____ my desk.
  a in   b next to   c between

5 _____ a cat on your bed.
  a Is   b There is   c There are

6 Jenny _____ brown hair and blue eyes.
  a is   b have   c has

7 Where is _____ phone?
  a my   b me   c I

8 How many sisters do you _____ ?
  a is   b have   c has

9 She has a big house, but _____ room is small.
  a her   b his   c our

| 8 |

3 Vocabulary

Underline the word that doesn't fit in each group.

1 chair	table	<u>kitchen</u>	desk
2 shower	bathtub	bed	sink
3 hallway	living room	dining room	sofa
4 green	blue	small	red
5 American	China	Indian	Colombian
6 bed	desk	computer	brown
7 Polish	Japan	Guatemala	Canada
8 fridge	stove	table	toilet
9 orange	yellow	sink	pink

| 8 |

How did you do?

Total: | 25 |

| 😊 | Very good 25 – 20 | 😐 | OK 19 – 16 | 😞 | Review Unit 1 again 15 or less |

2 Some of the rules

1 Remember and check

Read the sentences. Are they Westside Pool rules? Write ✓ (yes) or ✗ (no). Then check with the text on page 8 of the Student's Book.

1	Don't laugh.	✗		6	Close the doors in the pool area.	
2	Don't shout.			7	Don't jump into the pool.	
3	Run in the pool area.			8	Listen to the lifeguards.	
4	Don't run in the pool area.			9	Swim in the swimming lanes.	
5	Shout at the lifeguards.			10	Listen to your friends.	

2 Grammar

✱ Imperatives

a Make the imperatives negative.

1 Jump!   _Don't jump!_   3 Close the door! ....   5 Write an email. ....

2 Run! ....   4 Open the window. ....   6 Come in! ....

✱ Adverbs of frequency

b Make sentences from the information in the table.

✓✓✓✓ = always	✓✓✓ = usually	✓✓ = often
✓ = sometimes	✗✗ = hardly ever	✗✗✗✗ = never

	Louisa	Ben	Sue
get up early	✓✓✓	✓✓	✓✓✓✓
read a book	✗✗✗✗	✓✓	✓✓✓
listen to music	✓✓	✗✗	✓
go to the movies	✗✗	✓	✗✗✗✗

1 Ben _often gets up early._ ....

2 Louisa ....

3 Sue ....

4 Ben ....

5 Louisa ....

6 Sue ....

7 Ben ....

8 Louisa ....

9 Sue ....

10 Ben ....

11 Louisa ....

12 Sue ....

✱ Object pronouns

c Complete the table with object pronouns.

I	you	he	she	it	we	you	they
me	....	....	....	it	....	you	....

d <u>Underline</u> the correct words.

1 Nellie always tells _it / me_ about her day.

2 Jim listens to music every day. He likes _them / it_.

3 What do you want? I can help _you / her_.

4 Where is Mary? Maybe you should call _him / her_.

5 Our grandparents often give _us / it_ presents.

6 Mike always read books. He loves _them / it_.

✳ Can/can't for ability

e Complete the sentences. Use *can/can't* and a verb from the box.

> run ~~read~~ sing swim write

1 I like long books. I _can read_ fast.
2 Julia _____ well, but she can play the piano.
3 Look! Our dog _____ fast!
4 Let's go to the pool. _____ you _____?
5 My little brother _____ his name. He's only three years old.

✳ There is / there are (negative and questions) + a/an/any

f Complete the questions with *Is there a* or *Are there any*. Then look at the table and answer the questions.

1 _Are there any_ movie theaters in Jacksonville? _Yes, there are._
2 _____ dance clubs? _____
3 _____ subway station? _____
4 _____ shoe store? _____
5 _____ cafés? _____
6 _____ train station? _____
7 _____ post offices? _____
8 _____ bookstores? _____

Jacksonville	
post offices	2
dance clubs	0
train station	1
movie theaters	3
bookstores	0
cafés	4
shoe store	1
subway stations	0

③ Vocabulary

✳ Activity verbs

a Write the letters *a, e, i, o, u* or *y* in the blanks to complete the activity words.

1 o p e n
2 c l _ s _
3 r _ n
4 s w _ m
5 l _ s t _ n
6 r _ _ d
7 j _ m p
8 l _ _ g h
9 c r _
10 w r _ t _
11 s h _ _ t
12 s m _ l _

b Use some of the words from Exercise 3a to complete the sentences.

1 I _write_ new words in my notebook.
2 I _____ a book every week.
3 My parents never _____ to music.
4 It's sometimes hot in my room at night, so I _____ the window.
5 On the weekend, we go to the beach and _____ in the ocean.
6 I can walk in these shoes, but I can't _____ in them!
7 Our teacher's funny. We always _____ a lot in her class.
8 I'm cold! Can you _____ the door, please?

✳ Places

c Find seven places in the wordsnake and (circle) them.

caféntrainstationbookstoremovietheaterpostofficeshoestoreclothingstore

d Match the places from Exercise 3c with the pictures.

1 .... *post office* ....
2 ....
3 ....
4 ....
5 ....
6 ....
7 ....

① ② ③ ④

⑤ ⑥ ⑦

✳ Time

e Write each time two ways.

1   *1:00*   *one o'clock*

2 ....

3 ....

4 ....

5 ....

6 ....

✳ Clothes and prices

f Write the names of the clothes and the prices.

① $34.50
② $42
③ $15.75
④ $70
⑤ $9.40
⑥ $64.99

	Item	Price
1	*shirt*	*thirty-four dollars and fifty cents*
2		
3		
4		
5		
6		

4 Pronunciation

✶ *can/can't*

a ▶ CD3 T11 Listen and check *can* or *can't*.

	Can	Can't
1		✓
2		
3		
4		
5		
6		

b ▶ CD3 T12 Listen and write *can* or *can't*.

1 Jodi ___can___ run, but she _____ run fast.

2 I _____ draw, but I _____ paint.

3 _____ you swim? I _____ .

4 David _____ play the piano. He _____ play soccer.

5 Everyday English

Complete the expressions.

1 A: _____ don't we listen to music?
   B: OK.

2 A: I have two tickets to a concert.
   B: _____ ? Let's go!

3 You _____ are great! Thanks for the help.

4 A: This pizza is terrible.
   B: It's not that _____ .

5 A: Read 20 pages for class tomorrow.
   B: That's not _____ !

6 A: Let's go to the café.
   B: It's too _____ for that now.

6 Study help

✶ Spelling

Some words are pronounced the same in English, but they are spelled differently. They also have different meanings. These words are easy to confuse. Remembering these words will help you when you write in English.

it's = it is
its = the possessive adjective form of *it*

they're = they are
their = the possessive adjective form of *they*
there = use with *there is* and *there are*

you're = you are
your = the possessive adjective form of *you*

our = the possessive adjective form of *we*
hour = 60 minutes

buy = to purchase something
bye = short for *goodbye*

two = 2
too = also

Circle the correct words.

1 (*They're / There / Their*) in my class.

2 I have a new dog. (*It's / Its*) name is Muffin.

3 (*Bye / Buy*) me that sweater, please.

4 You can come to (*our / hour*) house for dinner.

5 It's (*two / too*) thirty.

6 Is Tom (*you're / your*) brother?

Write the words that are easy to confuse and their meanings in your notebook. You might want to write a sentence with each word to help you remember how to use it. Add others to your notebook as you learn more English.

Skills in mind

7 Listen

▶ **CDX TXX** Listen to Mr. Trenton give instructions to students. Number the rules in the order you hear them.

8 Read

Read the rules for tic-tac-toe. Then number the game in the correct order. Who won the game — Xs or Os?

Tic-tac-toe is an easy and fun game.
- Play with two people.
- Draw a grid on a piece of paper.
- One person is X and one person is O.
- Take turns.
- X goes first.
- X: Draw an X in any spot.
- O: Draw an O in any spot.
- Try to get three Xs or three Os in a row.
- Try to stop the other person from getting three in a row.
- When you get three in a row, draw a line through your three Xs or Os. You win!
- Sometimes no one wins. We say "the cat" wins these games. Draw a big C through the grid.
- Start a new game!

READING TIP

There are many ways to practice reading in English outside the classroom. Don't start with something long, like a book. Start with something small. Make it fun and easy. Here are some ideas for reading practice outside the class:

- Read rules to a game. You can look on the Internet.
- Read menus in English from restaurants.
- Read flyers from stores.
- Read short magazine articles.
- Read "top ten" lists on the Internet or in magazines.
- Read short newspaper articles or even captions under photos.
- Read comic strips in newspapers.

See if you can find and read rules to a game on the Internet or read something else from the idea list at home.

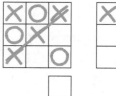   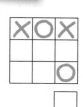

Unit check

1 Fill in the blanks

Complete the text with words in the box.

bookstore always dresses run $10 ~~can~~ can't shirts 9:00 him

Delilah and Candy are sisters, but they are very different. Delilah ___can___ draw and paint well, but she
¹_____ play sports. Candy can play soccer and tennis, but she isn't good at art. Delilah has a lot of
skirts and ²_____ . Candy only has pants and ³_____ . Delilah gets up at 7:00 every day. Candy
sleeps until ⁴_____ . Delilah likes the library because she can read a lot of books for free. Candy has
a lot of books that she gets at the ⁵_____ . She usually pays about ⁶_____ for each book.
They have one thing in common. They ⁷_____ tell their brother what to do. They tell ⁸_____ ,
"Close the door! Be quiet! Don't ⁹_____ !"

☐ 9

2 Choose the correct answers

Circle the correct answer: a, b or c.

1 _____ the door.
  a To close b Closes c Close

2 Jennifer is _____ late to class.
  a now b never c no

3 Please call _____ tonight.
  a me b I c you

4 Simon can paint, but he _____ draw.
  a can b can't c not

5 _____ a train station in your city?
  a Is there b There is c Are there

6 Are there _____ dance clubs on this street?
  a a b an c any

7 It's Jim's birthday. Let's give _____ a present.
  a us b her c him

8 _____ jump into the pool!
  a Do b Don't c Help

9 There _____ a hotel here.
  a isn't b aren't c any

☐ 8

3 Vocabulary

Vocabulary: Activity verb, places, time, clothes, money and prices
Underline the correct words.

1 Denny's shirt is pink, and his *pants* / *dress* are black.

2 Don't *run* / *close* in the hallway.

3 It's *seven* / *seven thirty* o'clock.

4 That sweater is seventeen *dollars* / *cent*.

5 Do you have a green *sweater* / *shoes*?

6 There are two dance *stores* / *clubs* in our city.

7 *Read* / *Listen* 20 pages tonight.

8 Is there a post *office* / *station* on Park Street?

9 The scarf is nine dollars and *fifty* / *one* cents.

☐ 8

How did you do?

Total: ☐ 25

😊	Very good 25 – 20	😐	OK 19 – 16	😞	Review Unit 2 again 15 or less

3 Free time

1 Remember and check

Read the sentences about Kellie Lenamond. <u>Underline</u> the correct words. Then check with the text on page 16 of the Student's Book.

1 Kellie *is* / *isn't* from the United States.
2 She has *five* / *six* beehives.
3 She has about *360,000* / *630,000* bees.
4 On a typical day, Kellie feeds the bees *before* / *after* dinner.
5 She feeds her bees a mixture of *sugar* / *honey* and water.
6 Her bees produce about *30* / *35* liters of honey.
7 In the summer, Kellie sells the *bees* / *honey*.
8 Kellie's friends *are* / *aren't* scared of the bees.

2 Grammar

✱ Simple present (affirmative and negative; questions and short answers)

a Complete the sentences. Use the simple present form of the verbs in parentheses.

1 I *love* (love) music.
2 John _____ (study) in his bedroom.
3 Linda's brothers _____ (get up) at 7:30.
4 My mother _____ (write) children's books.
5 Our dog _____ (sleep) in the yard.
6 Mom and Dad _____ (drive) to the supermarket on Saturday.
7 We really _____ (like) the new café.
8 Louise _____ (get) nervous before a test at school.

b Look at the pictures. Complete the sentences with the negative form of the verbs.

1 He plays tennis, but he *doesn't play soccer* .
2 My aunt likes dogs, but she _____ .
3 I read newspapers, but I _____ .
4 My parents watch movies, but they _____ .
5 Matt likes trains, but he _____ .

c Complete the questions and answers.

1 A: *Do* you *know* the answer to this question?
   B: No, *I don't* . I don't know any of the answers!
2 A: _____ you _____ to the radio?
   B: No, I don't. But I listen to music on my computer.
3 A: _____ going to the beach?
   B: No, she doesn't. But she likes going to the movies.
4 A: _____ science at school?
   B: Yes, _____ . They study biology and physics.
5 A: _____ English?
   B: Yes, he does. He speaks French and Italian, too.
6 A: Where _____ you _____ ?
   B: I live in an apartment in Chicago.
7 A: When _____ your brothers _____ to the gym?
   B: They go there on Friday afternoons.
8 A: What _____ to work?
   B: She wears a brown and white uniform.

d Complete the dialogue. Use the simple present form of the verbs in parentheses.

Ben: What __do__ you usually __do__ (do) on the weekend, Andy?

Andy: Oh, my weekends are always the same. I [1]_____ (meet) my friends on Friday night, and we [2]_____ (go) to the movies.

Ben: Where [3]_____ you _____ (go) after the movie?

Andy: To our favorite café. We [4]_____ (drink) coffee or hot chocolate there. Usually we [5]_____ (not go) home before 11 o'clock.

Ben: And what about Saturday?

Andy: On Saturday I [6]_____ (get up) early. I [7]_____ (play) games on my sister's computer. It's OK, because she [8]_____ (not get up) before 10:30 on Saturday.

Ben: [9]_____ your sister _____ (work)?

Andy: Yes, she [10]_____ (work) in a store, but she [11]_____ (not like) her job.

Ben: Oh, I see. And what else do you do on the weekend?

Andy: Well, my friends often [12]_____ (come) to my house on Saturday afternoon. On Sunday I [13]_____ (not go) out. I [14]_____ (do) my homework.

Ben: Yeah, me too.

3 # Vocabulary
✳ Hobbies and interests

a Design a logo (a simple picture) for each activity.

①	②	③	④
swimming	playing computer games	running	going to the movies

⑤	⑥	⑦	⑧
reading	painting	listening to music	dancing

b Match the words with the activities from Exercise 3a.

1 pool   _swimming_   5 dance clubs   _____
2 book   _____   6 picture   _____
3 sneakers   _____   7 MP3 player   _____
4 computer   _____   8 theater   _____

c **Vocabulary bank** Complete phrases 1–8 with the words in the box. Then match them with the pictures.

> making   keeping   taking care of   doing   hanging out
> ~~going~~   collecting   drawing

1 _going_ for walks   5 _____ models
2 _____ puzzles   6 _____ with friends
3 _____ a dog   7 _____ pictures
4 _____ stickers or coins   8 _____ a journal

4 Grammar

★ like + -ing

a Write the *-ing* form of the verbs.

1 play *playing*   3 go _____   5 study _____   7 swim _____

2 dance _____   4 smile _____   6 fly _____   8 run _____

b Complete the sentences about the people in the pictures. Use *like/enjoy*, *not like/enjoy*, *love* or *hate*.

 ①  ②  ③  ④

 ⑤  ⑥  ⑦  ⑧

1 Greg and Rachel *like going to the beach* .

2 David _____ .

3 Chris _____ .

4 Claire _____ .

5 Janet and Philip _____ .

6 Diane and George _____ .

7 Marco and Paola _____ .

8 Kelly _____ .

c Write six true sentences about activities that you and your friends enjoy or don't enjoy. Use *like/enjoy*, *not like/enjoy*, *love* or *hate*.

I love taking photos. Gina and Joe don't like writing letters.

1 _____ .

2 _____ .

3 _____ .

4 _____ .

5 _____ .

6 _____ .

5 Pronunciation

✱ /n/ (man) and /ŋ/ (song)

a ▶ CD3 T14 Listen and <u>underline</u> the words you hear. Then listen again and repeat.

1	<u>listen</u>	listening
2	open	opening
3	Ron	wrong
4	wins	wings
5	spin	spring
6	go in	going
7	come in	coming
8	drive in	driving

b ▶ CD3 T15 Listen and write the word or words you hear in the spaces.

1 Ann _____ every weekend.

2 I enjoy _____ another language.

3 We _____ every day.

4 Let's go _____ .

5 We usually _____ the summer.

6 Culture in mind

Complete the summary about Tonya, Elsa and Mark's school with the words in the box. Then check with the text on page 20 of the Student's Book.

basketball Japanese ~~arts~~ camera dance
science environment sports after school

LaGuardia High School is a performing ___arts___ school in New York City. Students study academic subjects like English, math, health and [1] _____ . They also study languages like Spanish or [2] _____ . What makes LaGuardia special is that students also take classes like music, theater or [3] _____ .

In addition to classes, there are also many activities for students [4] _____ . There are many clubs like a movie club, a knitting club, and an [5] _____ club. Tonya's favorite club is the [6] _____ club. There are also many [7] _____ for students. For example, students can play soccer, tennis or volleyball. Mark is on the [8] _____ team, and he enjoys playing with others.

LaGuardia is a great school for an education, performing arts and for other student interests.

7 Study help

✱ Vocabulary

In your Vocabulary notebook, organize new words into groups and list them under headings. Leave a lot of space at the bottom of each list so you can add other words later. For example:

Places in town		
Stores	**Public buildings**	**Other places**
shoe store	post office	theater
bookstore	library	café

Look at the words in the box. Group them in lists with headings. Can you add more words to each group?

movie theater ~~Sports~~ playing the piano ~~playing soccer~~ beach reading Music
Places dancing Other ~~Hobbies and interests~~ swimming painting

Hobbies and interests			
Sports	_____	_____	_____
playing soccer	_____	_____	_____
_____	_____	_____	_____
_____	_____	_____	_____

Skills in mind

8 Listen

▶CD3 T16 Listen to four people talking about their favorite activities. Match each person with two activities. Write numbers 1–8 in the boxes.

Sally ☐ ☐

Richard ☐ ☐

James ☐ ☐

Nadia 1 ☐

1 go to the movies
2 go to the swimming pool
3 talk to friends
4 play computer games
5 go dancing
6 play the guitar
7 write emails
8 ride a bicycle

9 Read

The boy in the picture is a student in Boston. He doesn't like sports, but he's very good at music. Is his name Adam, Matthew or Carlos? Read the information and fill in the table (✓ or ✗) to figure out the answer.

- Adam goes to a school near his home in Boston.
- Carlos plays soccer at school, but he doesn't really enjoy it.
- Matthew likes music, and he's good at playing the piano.
- Adam loves swimming, and he plays tennis on the weekend.
- Carlos sings and plays the guitar in the school band.
- Matthew loves living in Boston.
- Adam hates singing, and he doesn't play a musical instrument.
- Matthew enjoys riding his bike to school, but he doesn't like sports.
- Carlos lives in an apartment in Plymouth.

	lives in Boston	likes sports	plays music
Adam	✓		
Matthew			
Carlos			

The boy's name is _____ .

Unit check

1 Fill in the blanks

Complete the text with the words in the box.

watches   movies   different   doesn't   like   games   talking   person   ~~unusual~~   teaches

My friend Alan has an _unusual_ hobby. He loves old movies. We often go to the ¹_____ together on the weekend. We ²_____ watching modern movies, but Alan's favorite movies are the old black-and-white ones from the 1930s and 1940s. He ³_____ them and reads about them all the time. I really enjoy ⁴_____ to him about movies because he knows a lot about them, and he ⁵_____ me a lot. Alan ⁶_____ play soccer, and he hates computer ⁷_____, so some people think he's a little strange. But it's good to be ⁸_____, and I think he's a very interesting ⁹_____ .

| | 9 |

2 Choose the correct answers

(Circle) the correct answer: a, b or c.

1 Danny _____ to go to the party.

  a want   b (wants)   c wanting

2 I _____ emails on my computer.

  a run   b write   c talk

3 I really _____ Alison. She's a very good friend.

  a love   b hate   c don't like

4 Our classes _____ at 8:50.

  a start   b starts   c starting

5 David _____ your aunt and uncle.

  a know   b knows   c knowing

6 My friends _____ read a lot of books.

  a does   b doesn't   c don't

7 Angela and Dylan enjoy _____ pictures.

  a paint   b to paint   c painting

8 Playing the guitar is my favorite _____ .

  a game   b hobby   c sport

9 All the students in our school _____ English.

  a listen   b teach   c learn

| | 8 |

3 Vocabulary

Complete the sentences with the words in the box.

theater   ~~swimming~~   keeping   running
playing   dancing   painting   writing   hobbies

1 We go _swimming_ at the pool in our town.

2 I go _____ in the park every morning before breakfast.

3 He loves _____ the guitar.

4 TV is OK, but I really enjoy watching movies at the movie _____ .

5 Do you have any _____ ?

6 I don't really enjoy _____ emails.

7 Her hobby is _____ bees.

8 My sister loves _____ pictures.

9 I love _____ , but only when the music's good!

| | 8 |

How did you do?

Total: | 25 |

| 😊 | Very good 25 – 20 | 😐 | OK 19 – 16 | 🙁 | Review Unit 3 again 15 or less |

4 Helping other people

1 Remember and check

Read the sentences about Mike Coleman. Circle the correct answer: a, b or c. Then check with the text on page 22 of the Student's Book.

1 Mike is _____ before he studies to be a teacher.
   a taking a vacation
   b becoming a nurse
   c taking a year off

2 He is _____ in Namibia.
   a working in a hospital
   b teaching in a school
   c learning to be a doctor

3 He _____ for his work.
   a needs a lot of help
   b doesn't get any money
   c gets a lot of money

4 He _____ in Namibia.
   a is staying for six months
   b is living in a big house
   c is enjoying his life

5 When he finishes his work, he wants to _____ .
   a go home
   b travel for three weeks
   c learn about life in southern Africa

2 Grammar

✱ Present continuous for activities happening now

a Complete the phone message with the correct form of *be* (affirmative or negative).

b Complete the dialogues. Use the present continuous form.

1 A: Sorry, I can't talk to you. I'm busy.
   B: Oh? What / you / do? *What are you doing?*

2 A: Hannah's TV is on in her room.
   B: Oh? What / she / watch _____ ?

3 A: Paul, you / get dressed _____ ?
   B: Yes, I'm in my room. I / get / ready _____ ?

4 A: Chloe, I need the phone. Who / you / call _____ ?
   B: Alex. He / help / me / with my homework _____ .

5 A: Brianna, what's the matter? Why / you / cry _____ ?
   B: I / not cry! I / laugh _____ !
      This movie's really funny!

Hi, John. This is Patrick. I *'m* sitting on the bus. We [1] _____ coming to Seattle, and it [2] _____ raining, of course! The streets are really busy today, and we [3] _____ moving at all right now. Karen is here somewhere, but I can't see her. She [4] _____ sitting near me. Anyway, I [5] _____ calling to ask for some help. I know you [6] _____ studying at the library now, but when you finish, can you pick us up from the bus station? Mom and Dad [7] _____ working today, so they can't come and get us. Call me back. Bye.

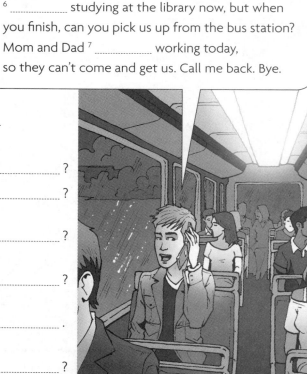

c What's happening in the pictures? Write two sentences in the present continuous for each picture. More than one answer is possible.

1 *Jack and Linda are eating pizza.*   *Harry is drinking coffee.*

2 _____ .   _____ .

3 _____ .   _____ .

4 _____ .   _____ .

5 _____ .   _____ .

6 _____ .   _____ .

✳ Simple present vs. present continuous

d Match the two parts of the sentences.

1 My friend works   a for their test now.
2 She's helping her mother   b at six o'clock every morning.
3 I enjoy going   c to me.
4 They're studying   d at the supermarket on Saturday.
5 You aren't listening   e cook dinner.
6 Andrew leaves home   f to the movies.

e Complete the sentences. Use the simple present or present continuous form of the verbs in parentheses.

1 My father __starts__ (start) work at nine o'clock every morning.

2 Sorry, Mike, I can't talk to you now. I'm busy. I _____ (do) my homework.

3 My cousins _____ usually _____ (not stay) with us in the summer.

4 Julia hardly ever _____ (go) to the beach.

5 My brother _____ (not use) the computer right now.

6 Be quiet, Amy! We _____ (watch) this show.

7 Jane isn't here right now. She _____ (shop) at the mall.

8 What _____ you _____ (do) after school on Friday?

9 _____ Steve and Matt _____ (play) basketball now?

10 Can you help me? I _____ (not understand) this question.

③ Vocabulary

✳ Housework

Cook ☐
Go shopping ☐ 1
Do the dishes ☐
Do the laundry ☐
Wash the windows ☐
Clean the bedrooms ☐

a Maria's mother is in the hospital. Maria has a list of jobs to do in the house, and her friends are helping her.

▶ **CD3 T17** Listen to the sounds. Write numbers 1–6 next to the jobs on the list.

b Maria's mother is calling from the hospital. Look at the pictures, and write what Maria says to her on the phone.

1 We're fine, Mom. Stephanie _is going shopping._

2 Tim _____ .

3 Lisa and Susan _____ _____ .

4 René and Marina _____ _____ .

5 Tony _____ _____ .

6 Kate and Richard _____ _____ .

c 🔘 **Vocabulary bank** Fill in the word puzzle and find the mystery word.

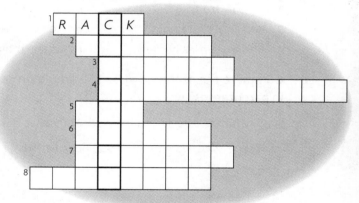

| ¹R | A | C | K | | | |

1 a CD _rack_

2 a _____

3 a _____

4 _____

5 a _____

6 a clothes _____

7 some _____

8 a _____

4 Pronunciation

✳ /ɔr/ (*more*) and /ər/ (*girl*)

a ▶CD3 T18 Listen and repeat.

1 bored	bird
2 born	burn
3 wore	work
4 short	shirt

b ▶CD3 T19 Listen and write the words in the lists.

> ~~more~~   door   be<u>fore</u>   <u>lear</u>ning   ~~girl~~
> <u>wor</u>king   uni<u>form</u>   <u>bir</u>thday

/ɔr/	/ər/
more	*girl*

c ▶CD3 T20 <u>Underline</u> the words with the /ɔr/ sound. (Circle) the words with the /ər/ sound. Then listen, check and repeat.

1 The <u>information</u> is on the (computer.)
2 I was born in Turkey.
3 Her parents are working in Portugal.
4 The girls are organizing their research.
5 Laura was early for work this morning.

5 Everyday English

(Circle) the correct words.

1 A: Excuse me. Are you the man who takes care of the gorilla?
   B: That's *it* / (*right*). Why?

2 A: This movie is terrible!
   B: *See?* / *Look?* I told you. My sister saw it, and she thought it was bad, too!

3 A: Jack? Can you help me with my homework?
   B: Sorry, Midge. It's not my *problem* / *right*.

4 A: We're late! Come *in* / *on*, Sally.
   B: All right, I'm coming!

5 A: This chocolate's very expensive!
   B: I know! It's really good, *though* / *so*!

6 A: Alex called me again last night!
   B: *So* / *And* what? He calls all the girls. It doesn't mean you're special!

6 Study help

✳ Grammar and vocabulary

When you learn new words, try to identify them as parts of speech (nouns, verbs, etc.). This can help you remember how to use them in a sentence.

a (Circle) the verbs and <u>underline</u> the nouns.

1 I (use) my <u>computer</u> a lot.
2 Gemma plays in the orchestra.
3 Some students bring sandwiches and eat them at school.
4 We usually walk, but sometimes we catch the bus.

b In your Vocabulary notebook, you can list nouns and verbs together.

Fill in the lists with the words in the box. Can you add two more to each group?

> ~~English~~   ~~study~~   ~~class~~   test   art
> teach   write   uniform   geography

SCHOOL

Nouns   Verbs

Subjects   Other nouns

English	*class*	*study*

7 Read and Listen

a Read part of the interview with Mike from page 22 of the Student's Book. Complete it with as many words as you can.

Interviewer: Good morning, and welcome to the Morning Show on WZVR. This morning we're ____talking____ about volunteer work. On our phone line, we have Mike Coleman, from Omaha, Nebraska. Right now he's in Namibia. Good morning, Mike.

Mike: Hi, Carol.

Interviewer: What are you ¹_____ there in Namibia?

Mike: I'm working as a ²_____ in a hospital. I'm here for two months. I help the doctors and nurses. You know, I ³_____ things and get things for them, talk to the patients, that kind of thing.

Interviewer: And what are you doing right now?

Mike: I'm ⁴_____ breakfast. We always eat breakfast at about ⁵_____ o'clock. Then we go to the hospital.

Interviewer: Do you ⁶_____ your own breakfast?

Mike: Yes, we do. And lunch and dinner, too! Six of us live here ⁷_____ and we do all of our own housework.

Interviewer: Really?

Mike: Yes. We do all the ⁸_____ and cleaning. We ⁹_____ our own clothes, too. There's no washing machine here!

b ▶ **CD3 T21** Listen and check your answers.

8 Write

Read David's email. Then write an email in reply to him. Tell him what's happening in your home right now.

> ⬤⬤⬤
>
> Hi!
>
> How are you? I'm not doing anything very interesting. I'm sitting in my room, and I'm listening to the radio. They're playing old 1980s songs right now. The cat's here, too. She's sleeping on my bed. My sisters are watching TV in the living room, and they're laughing like crazy. Mom is cooking dinner in the kitchen. Dad isn't here right now. He's working tonight. It's raining here, and I'm feeling bored. What about you? What are you doing? Write and tell me what's happening.
>
> David

WRITING TIP

Brainstorming

Before you start to write, "brainstorm" ideas.

- Think of *all* the things that are happening now, and make quick notes on a piece of paper without stopping. Write words or phrases in English where you can, but it's fine to use words in your own language, too.

- Don't worry if some ideas aren't very important, or if they are mixed up and out of order. The main thing is to write ideas.

After brainstorming, you can look at your notes, cross out ideas you don't want to use and start to put the others in order.

Unit check

1 Fill in the blanks

Complete the text with the words in the box.

is works grocery shopping ~~go out~~ now morning hate up right the

Ethan Fletcher and his sister Olivia usually _go out_ with their friends on Saturday, but this [1]_____
they're busy at home. They're cleaning [2]_____ after a big party for Olivia's birthday. Right [3]_____
Olivia is doing [4]_____ dishes in the kitchen, and Ethan [5]_____ cleaning the bathroom.
They [6]_____ housework, so they aren't having a lot of fun [7]_____ now. Their parents aren't
at home. Mrs. Fletcher always [8]_____ on Saturday mornings, and Mr. Fletcher is going [9]_____
at the supermarket.

▮ 9

2 Choose the correct answers

(Circle) the correct answer: a, b or c.

1 I always listen to the radio when I _____ the dishes.
   a (do) b help c work

2 Marco is _____ the windows for his grandmother.
   a doing b washing c ironing

3 Steve is in Turkey now. _____ in Istanbul.
   a He stay b He stays c He's staying

4 Diane and her sister _____ playing tennis right now.
   a isn't b aren't c don't

5 It _____ right now, but it's very cold.
   a snows b doesn't snow c isn't snowing

6 Who are those boys over there? _____ them?
   a You know b Do you know
   c Are you knowing

7 A: Is Alyssa doing her homework? B: No, she _____ .
   a isn't b doesn't c don't

8 It's a nice day. _____ to go to the beach?
   a I like b You want c Do you want

9 I visit my aunt and uncle _____ a month.
   a two b twice c second

▮ 8

3 Vocabulary

Complete the sentences with the phrases in the box.

cook do the dishes take a nap do the laundry clean up wash the windows ~~do the housework~~ go grocery shopping iron the clothes

1 The house is a mess. It's time to _do the housework_ .

2 All my clothes are dirty. It's time to _____ .

3 There's no food in the fridge. It's time to _____ .

4 We're all hungry, and we want our dinner. It's time to _____ .

5 My shirts are clean, but I can't wear them yet. It's time to _____ .

6 The plates are dirty. It's time to _____ .

7 There are things all over the floor in my bedroom. It's time to _____ .

8 I'm in my bedroom, but I can't see outside. It's time to _____ .

9 I'm really tired after doing all the housework. It's time to _____ !

▮ 8

How did you do?

Total: ▮ 25

 Very good 25 – 20	OK 19 – 16	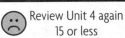 Review Unit 4 again 15 or less

5 Who's your hero?

1 Remember and check

Read the sentences about Erin Brockovich. Write *T* (true) or *F* (false). Then check with the text on page 30 of the Student's Book.

1 Erin Brockovich studied law in college.   [F]

2 Erin's job at the law company was to help sick people.   [ ]

3 Erin found that a lot of sick people lived near a big Pacific Gas and Electric factory.   [ ]

4 People were sick because there was chromium in their drinking water.   [ ]

5 Each of the 600 sick people got $1 million from the company.   [ ]

6 Julia Roberts played Erin Brockovich in a movie.   [ ]

2 Grammar

✱ Simple past: *be*

a Underline the correct words.

1 There *was* / *were* some interesting shows on TV yesterday.

2 My father *was* / *were* really angry with me last night.

3 Our test was very difficult, so we *were* / *weren't* very happy.

4 *You were* / *Were you* in the library yesterday?

5 One of my brothers *was* / *were* in Brazil last year.

6 We enjoyed the meal last night. The food *was* / *wasn't* really good.

7 *Was* / *Were* they on vacation in Greece?

8 Where *was* / *were* Richard last night?

b ▶CD3 T22 Read the dialogue between Lauren and her grandmother. Fill in the blanks with *was*, *were*, *wasn't* or *weren't*. Then listen and check your answers.

Grandma: Oh, look at this old record!

Lauren: Who is it, Grandma?

Grandma: It's Buddy Holly. He __was__ my favorite singer when I [1] _____ young!

Lauren: [2] _____ he British?

Grandma: No, he [3] _____ American.

Lauren: I don't know him at all.

Grandma: No, of course you don't. He died in 1959. And he [4] _____ very old. He [5] _____ only 22.

Lauren: What happened?

Grandma: Well, he [6] _____ in a small airplane, in the winter. Two other singers [7] _____ in the plane with him. The plane crashed, and they all died.

Lauren: Oh, that's terrible.

Grandma: Yes, I [8] _____ very sad. I cried all day!

Lauren: Tell me more about him.

Grandma: Well, *Peggy Sue* and *That'll Be the Day* [9] _____ his famous songs in the 1950s. But they [10] _____ my favorites. My favorite Buddy Holly song [11] _____ *Everyday*. Do you want to hear it?

Lauren: OK, Grandma. Play it for me!

✱ Simple past: regular verbs

c Write the simple past form of the verbs. Think carefully about the spelling. Is it -ed? -d? -ied? or double consonant + -ed?

1 enjoy   *enjoyed*
2 hate   ....
3 climb   ....
4 stay   ....
5 listen   ....
6 cry   ....

7 plan   ....
8 decide   ....
9 talk   ....
10 stop   ....
11 study   ....
12 wash   ....

d Look at the pictures and complete the sentences. Use six of the simple past verbs in Exercise 2c.

1 I *hated* eating vegetables when I was a child.

2 We .... all the windows on Saturday. It was hard work.

3 Tim .... to some good music last night.

4 The baby .... when I picked him up.

5 The car .... because the light was red.

6 Andrea .... to Peter on the phone yesterday.

e Complete the sentences. Use the negative form of the verbs in the box.

> study   ~~visit~~   speak   do
> answer   cook

1 Kevin *didn't visit* his grandmother yesterday, but he called her at the hospital.

2 I asked him a question, but he .... me.

3 I .... last night because we decided to eat out.

4 Sophie was really angry. She .... to us for three days!

5 Lisa and Sam .... yesterday because their classes ended last week.

6 I washed all the clothes, but I .... the dishes.

f Complete the paragraph. Use the simple past form of the verbs in parentheses.

My aunt and uncle were here last weekend. They *didn't stay* (not stay) at our apartment. They ¹ .... (stay) in a hotel downtown. Their room was nice, but my aunt ² .... (not like) the food. She ³ .... (visit) us on Saturday, and she and Mom ⁴ .... (talk) for the whole afternoon. My uncle ⁵ .... (not want) to sit inside, so he and I ⁶ .... (walk) to the stadium to watch the soccer game. But we ⁷ .... (not have) a very good time because our team ⁸ .... (not play) well, and at 3:30 it ⁹ .... (start) to rain.

3 Vocabulary
✳ Multi-word verbs (1)

a Look at the pictures. What are the people saying? Write numbers 1–4 in the boxes.

1 Get out!
2 Get in!
3 Come down!
4 Climb up!

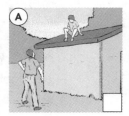   

b We can use an object pronoun, like *it* or *them*, with some two-word verbs. The pronoun goes <u>between</u> the two parts of the verb. Look at the pictures and make sentences. Use words from each box.

put on   take off   ~~pick up~~   put down

it   them

① *Pick it up!*

②

③

④

c Can you find multi-word verbs to complete these sentences? Choose a word from each box, and then use your dictionary to check.

sit   go   grows   Turn   ~~try~~

up   off   ~~on~~   out   down

1 I like these pants, but I want to _try_ them _on_ before I buy them.

2 John's little sister wants to be a doctor when she _____ .

3 _____ the TV! All the shows are terrible tonight.

4 Let's _____ on this seat and have our lunch.

5 Sorry, the boys aren't at home. They always _____ on Friday nights.

d **Vocabulary bank** Complete the sentences with *up*, *down*, *on* or *off*.

1 In some countries, kids stand _up_ when the teacher comes into the classroom.

2 On Sundays I get _____ at about ten o'clock.

3 It was difficult to see, so we turned _____ the lights.

4 Come and sit _____ on the sofa next to me.

5 The movie on TV was really boring, so I turned it _____ and started reading.

6 I'm really tired. I'm going to lie _____ in my room for an hour.

7 When the bus came it was full, so I didn't get _____ it. I waited ten minutes for the next bus.

8 Mom! The dog's sitting on my bed. Tell it to get _____ !

4 Pronunciation

❋ -ed endings

a ▶CD3 T23 How many syllables are there in these simple past verbs? Write the number 1, 2 or 3. Then listen, check and repeat.

1	closed	_1_	6	decided	....
2	watched	....	7	walked	....
3	needed	....	8	studied	....
4	started	....	9	planned	....
5	discovered	....	10	worked	....

b ▶CD3 T24 Listen and repeat the sentences.

1 She wanted a salad.
2 They watched a good movie.
3 He walked a long way.
4 We visited our friends.
5 I hated that book!
6 She climbed the hill.
7 We decided to go home.
8 He started to read.

5 Culture in mind

a Match the names and the descriptions. Then check on page 34 of the Student's Book.

1 Mount Rushmore
2 Simón Bolívar
3 Martin Luther King Jr.
4 the Memorial Fountain
5 Tom Jobim
6 Grauman's Chinese Theatre

a an American civil rights leader in the United States
b a Brazilian musician
c a place that honors four U.S. presidents
d a memorial in London for Princess Diana
e a South American leader
f a theater in Hollywood with memorials to movie stars

b Complete the text with the words in the box.

forget unforgettable memories memory ~~remember~~ memorials

We always want to _remember_ our heroes. We do different things to make sure that we don't ¹ .... the amazing people who did ² .... things when they were alive.

There are many kinds of ³ .... : statues, monuments, paintings and so on. They all help to keep famous and important people alive in our ⁴ .... Tourists often go to see them, and they take photographs. When they go home, they will have great ⁵ .... of their visit.

6 Study help

❋ Vocabulary

There are lots of multi-word verbs in English, formed with a normal verb + a small word like *up, down, in, out, on* or *off*. Often the multi-word verb has a very different meaning from the verb on its own. If you can't figure out the meaning, you can look up the multi-word verb in your dictionary.

a In your Vocabulary notebook, write the verbs with *up* and *down* from Exercises 8a and 8b in the Student's Book.

- Make two lists (*up* and *down* verbs).
- Add a phrase or sentence to show the meaning of each verb.
- Learn both parts of the verb together.

b Now look at this text and underline all the multi-word verbs.

Jenny wakes up at 6:30 when her alarm clock goes off. She turns on the light, gets up quickly, puts on her clothes and sneakers and sets off for a run before breakfast. Even when she gets cold and wet, Jenny keeps on running. She doesn't slow down, and she never gives up.

c Add any new verbs to your *up* and *down* lists. Can you figure out the meanings?

d Start new lists with *on, off, in* and *out*.

Skills in mind

7 Read

a Look at the pictures. What do you think the text is about?

IL FUMETTO DEL BRIVIDO
DIABOLIK
IL RE DEL TERRORE
ROMANZO COMPLETO
LIRE 150

Cover of Diabolik

Angela and Luciana Giussani, creators of Diabolik

AN ALL-ITALIAN HERO

1 Ask any Italian teenager about his or her favorite comic book hero, and what's the answer? Superman? Spider-Man? Batman? No, Italy's favorite hero is Diabolik.

2 Diabolik is an all-Italian hero. The idea came from two Italian sisters, Angela and Luciana Giussani, in 1962. But he isn't only popular in Italy. You can buy Diabolik comic books in many countries and read about him in a lot of different languages.

3 Who is Diabolik? Well, he is not the usual superhero. In fact, Diabolik is a thief. He takes things from rich people, and then he runs away.

4 He has a beautiful girlfriend called Eva. She helps him to plan his adventures, and they really love each other. Diabolik meets a lot of beautiful women, but Eva is the only girl for him.

5 Ginko, a police officer, often tries to catch Diabolik, but he is never successful. He always arrives too late to catch him.

b Read the text again. Write *T* (true) or *F* (false).

1 You can find Diabolik books all over the world. `T`

2 You need to know Italian to read the Diabolik books.

3 Diabolik is an unusual hero.

4 Diabolik doesn't have a girlfriend.

5 Ginko helps Diabolik plan his adventures.

6 Ginko never catches Diabolik.

c Find words in the text with these meanings.

1 a very strong and brave person in a book or movie (noun) ___*hero*___

2 very well liked (adjective) _____

3 person who takes other people's things (noun)

_____

4 with a lot of money (adjective) _____

5 very good-looking (adjective) _____

READING TIP

If you're a fan of Diabolik or other comic book characters, you can get the books in English translations.

It's fun to practice your reading by following your own interests. For example, if you have a favorite hobby, or if you're interested in a musician, an actor or an athlete, you can:

- read about them in American magazines
- go to fan websites in English on the Internet
- find out what other teenagers are saying by going to Internet chat rooms.

If you have a computer at home, look up Diabolik on the Internet now, and see what you can find in English.

Unit check

1 Fill in the blanks

Complete the text with the words in the box.

| was | wasn't | weren't | didn't | born | trees | discovered | traveled | planned | ~~Last~~ |

Last month, my boyfriend and I [1] _____ 50 kilometers to visit Great Oaks. I was [2] _____ near there, and it was a beautiful forest when I [3] _____ a child. It was also a great place to see animals. We decided to take some sandwiches, and we [4] _____ to eat them next to the river.

But we [5] _____ enjoy the day. People were cutting down a lot of the [6] _____ to make a road, and it was very noisy. When we tried to swim in the river, we [7] _____ that it was dirty. And there [8] _____ any animals. We decided to go home early, and I [9] _____ happy at all.

| | 9 |

2 Choose the correct answers

(Circle) the correct answer: a, b or c.

1 It was cold, so she decided to put _____ her jacket.

   a (on) b off c down

2 I picked _____ the book and started to read it.

   a on b up c down

3 It's dangerous up there in that tree. Come _____ !

   a down b off c out

4 My grandmother _____ born in 1948.

   a is b was c were

5 A: Was Paul at school yesterday?

   B: No, he _____ .

   a wasn't b weren't c didn't

6 Marilyn Monroe _____ in 1962.

   a killed b died c born

7 Our aunt and uncle _____ us last month.

   a visit b visits c visited

8 We _____ tennis in the park this morning.

   a playd b played c plaied

9 I was tired, so I _____ get up early.

   a was b doesn't c didn't

| | 8 |

3 Vocabulary

Write the opposite of each word with the words in the box.

| take off | turn on | ~~get off~~ | forget | sit down | get in | go out | put down | come up |

1 get on   _get off_   4 get out _____   7 pick up _____

2 come down _____   5 remember _____   8 put on _____

3 turn off _____   6 stand up _____   9 stay at home _____

| | 8 |

How did you do?

Total: | 25 |

| :) Very good 25 – 20 | :| OK 19 – 16 | :(Review Unit 5 again 15 or less |

6 Making friends

1 Remember and check

Match the two parts of the sentences. Then check with the text on page 36 of the Student's Book.

1 The 1971 World Table Tennis Championship
2 American and Chinese players
3 An American player named Cowan
4 Cowan missed his bus, but
5 A Chinese player named Zhuang Zedong
6 Later, Cowan gave Zedong
7 The two men
8 Their friendship helped China and the United States

a didn't talk to each other.
b became friends.
c a T-shirt in return.
d was in Japan.
e to have a better relationship.
f he got on the Chinese bus instead.
g invited a Chinese player to play with him.
h gave Cowan a silk scarf.

2 Grammar

✱ Simple past: regular and irregular verbs

a Underline the correct words.

1 Did you like the movie? I *taught / thought / thank* it was terrible!
2 Tom *wanted / won / went* an omelette, but we didn't have any eggs.
3 I called Kate from the station and *seed / sayed / said* goodbye to her.
4 Thanks for the meal. We really *enjoy / enjoyed / enjoied* it.
5 The CD *was / wasn't / weren't* very expensive, so they decided to buy it.
6 Many years ago, my father *met / meeted / made* a man named George Jones.
7 After a month, the two girls *become / became / becomes* very good friends.
8 Last year, my sister *left / let / leaved* school and got a job.

b Complete the sentences. Use the simple past form of the verbs in the box.

give ~~eat~~ win meet have leave go come

1 We don't have any chocolate. You _ate_ it all yesterday!
2 My friends _____ the party at 11 o'clock and walked home.
3 The basketball championship this afternoon was a great game, and our team _____ !
4 After lunch on Sunday, Nick and Beth _____ for a walk in the park.
5 The teacher _____ to class late, but she still _____ us a lot of homework.
6 I _____ Paolo at one o'clock, and we _____ lunch together at the café.

c Read the sentences. Can you figure out the names of the six girls? Write the names in the boxes.

There were six girls in the 500-meter race.
Pat and two other girls got the medals.
Angela didn't finish the race.

Judy finished the race, but she didn't beat anyone.
Maria beat **Judy**, but she didn't get a medal.
Liz didn't win the silver medal.
Sandra wasn't the winner. Two girls beat her.

1 _____

3 _____

5 _____

6 _____

4 _____

2 _____

d Mei was a volunteer worker at the Beijing Olympic Games in 2008. Read the interview and write the questions.

Interviewer: _Did you get paid for your work?_ (get / paid for your work?)

Mei: No, I didn't. I was a volunteer.

Interviewer: ¹ _____ ? (meet / a famous athlete?)

Mei: Yes, I did. I met Michael Phelps.

Interviewer: ² _____ ? (speak to you?)

Mei: Yes, he did. We had a short conversation.

Interviewer: ³ _____
_____ ? (the volunteers / stay / in the Olympic village?)

Mei: No, they didn't. Only the athletes stayed there.

Interviewer: ⁴ _____ ? (work hard?)

Mei: Yes, we did, but it was fun.

Interviewer: ⁵ _____
_____ ? (people / enjoy / the Olympic Games?)

Mei: Yes, they did. They had a really great time.

e ▶CD3 T25 Read part of the dialogue from Exercise 8 on page 39 of the Student's Book. Fill in the simple past verbs. Then listen and check.

Jason: ___Did___ you ___see___ Friends Forever last night?

Louise: No, I didn't. What was it about?

Jason: Well, there were these two boys, Dan and Nick. They ¹ _____ really good friends, you know. And they ² _____ on the same soccer team. One day, their team ³ _____ a big game.

Louise: Uh huh. And what ⁴ _____ ?

Jason: Well, it wasn't a great start for Dan and Nick's team. At half time the score was 3–0 with the other team winning. But then Dan and Nick both ⁵ _____ to play really well. They ⁶ _____ two goals each. So, their team won 4–3. It was great, and the fans were excited.

Louise: OK.

Jason: So, the next issue of their school magazine ⁷ _____ an article with a big photo of Dan and Nick, and the headline ⁸ _____ , "Friends score double!"

Louise: So?

Jason: Well, Nick's father, Mr. Winter, ⁹ _____ the article. And he ¹⁰ _____ that Dan's last name was Stern, and he wasn't very happy.

Louise: Hang on a minute. I don't get it. When Nick's father ¹¹ _____ out about Dan's last name, he ¹² _____ happy?

Jason: That's right.

3 Vocabulary

✳ Time expressions (past)

a Fill in the crossword.

```
1 M A Y
        3
5           6
      7        8        9
10
              11
```

Across →

1 The month before June is _May_ .

3 It's Thursday today. Six days ago, it was

_____ .

5 It's 10:30 now. Half an _____ ago, it was
10 o'clock.

6 Now it's November. August was three

_____ ago.

8 Today is May 1. Two days ago, it was

_____ 29.

10 It's 2010 now. I met Paul four _____ ago,
in 2006.

11 It's Monday. Wednesday is the _____

after tomorrow.

Down ↓

1 Now it's July. Four months ago, it was _____ .

2 It's October 22 today. Two _____ ago,
it was October 8.

3 _____ is the month after January.

4 _____ was one day ago.

7 It's 8:15 now. _____ minutes ago it
was 8:05.

9 Today it's Sunday, November 4.
_____ Sunday it was October 28.

✳ Sports

b Match the sports with the pictures. Write the numbers 1–10 in the boxes.

1 skiing   2 surfing   3 basketball   4 ~~snowboarding~~   5 swimming   6 cycling   7 volleyball
8 hockey   9 skateboarding   10 tennis

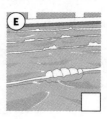

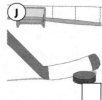

c **Vocabulary bank** In which picture in Exercise 3b can you see …

1 a helmet?   _C_   5 pads?   _____

2 a board?   _____   6 gloves?   _____

3 a racket?   _____   7 a pool?   _____

4 a stick?   _____   8 a court?   _____

4 Pronunciation

✱ Word stress

a ▶ **CD3 T26** These verbs all have two syllables. <u>Underline</u> the main stress. Is it on the first or the second syllable? Listen, check and repeat.

1 <u>ha</u>ppened
2 listened
3 began
4 arrived
5 studied
6 became

b ▶ **CD3 T27** Write the words in the lists. Then listen, check and repeat.

> ~~morning~~   ~~November~~   ~~yesterday~~   ~~because~~   July
> friendship   teenager   important   tonight   medal
> fantastic   athlete   volleyball   beginning   today
> exercise

Oo	oO	Ooo	oOo
morning	*because*	*yesterday*	*November*

5 Everyday English

Complete the dialogue with these expressions.

> let's just forget about it   ~~How about~~   to be honest
> I didn't mean to   I don't think so   on the other hand

Joanna: Mandy? [1] _____*How about*_____ going shopping this afternoon?

Mandy: No, [2] _____ , Joanna. I'm very busy, you know, with homework and things.

J: Oh, homework! You can do that tomorrow.

M: Well, I want to do it today. And [3] _____ , I don't really like shopping very much.

J: That's true. But [4] _____ , there are always a lot of boys there.

M: Boys? Joanna, I have a boyfriend! You know that!

J: Oh, no, did I say the wrong thing? Sorry, Mandy. [5] _____ .

M: Oh, [6] _____ , Joanna. Just go shopping, OK? Bye!

6 Study help

✱ Grammar

A lot of important and common verbs have an irregular simple past form.

- Make a list of irregular verbs, and add to it as you learn more. Write the base form and the simple past form together, in two columns.

- Learn both forms of the verb together. Read through your list regularly, and say the two forms aloud.

- Test yourself: cover one of the columns, and say or write the hidden verbs. Or you can make a set of cards with the base form on one side and the simple past on the other.

- To find the past form of an irregular verb, you can use the list on page 122 of the Student's Book. You can also look up the verb in your dictionary. If the past form is not listed, the verb has the regular -ed ending.

a Write the simple past form of these irregular verbs.

1 make _____*made*_____
2 get _____
3 come _____
4 see _____
5 take _____

b Here are some more irregular past forms. Can you write the base forms?

1 swam _____*swim*_____
2 forgot _____
3 spoke _____
4 drank _____
5 gave _____

7 Listen

▶ **CD3 T28** Listen to Lisa talking about three of her friends, Greg, Peter and Michael. Match the names with two pictures. Write the number 1, 2 or 3 in each box.

Lisa's friends: 1 Greg 2 Peter 3 Michael

How they met

What they do together

LISTENING TIP

Before you listen
- Look at the pictures. What do they show you about the people? Try to predict some things that Lisa will say about each picture.

While you listen
- First listen to the three parts of the recording, but don't write anything. Listen to Lisa's voice, and try to get the general idea of what she is saying.
- Now listen to part 1. What words do you hear that link the recording to picture C?
- Listen for words that are stressed. These are usually important words.
- When you have filled in all the boxes, listen again to check your answers.

8 Write

Write two paragraphs about a friend. Include this information:

Paragraph 1
- Where and when did you meet this person?
- When did you become friends?

Paragraph 2
- How often do you see your friend?
- What do you like doing together?

Unit check

1 Fill in the blanks

Complete the text with the words in the box.

| was   ago   began   looked   became   surfing   ~~went~~   friendship   said   didn't |

When I was nine, I __went__ to Tampa with my grandparents. I liked [1]_____ , and the beaches were great, but I was lonely because I [2]_____ have any friends. One afternoon, I walked down the street behind our hotel. Suddenly, there [3]_____ a big brown dog in front of me. It [4]_____ at me with angry yellow eyes, and I [5]_____ to get nervous. Then an American girl came down the street. "It's OK," she [6]_____ to me. She shouted some words in English, and the dog went away. The girl's name was Chloe, and after this we [7]_____ good friends. That was six years [8]_____ , but I still write to Chloe. Our [9]_____ is very important to me.

☐ 9

2 Choose the correct answers

Circle the correct answer: a, b or c.

1 Good _____ players are usually tall.

   a skateboarding   b (basketball)   c skiing

2 For _____ , you need a bike.

   a gymnastics   b surfing   c cycling

3 _____ is a winter sport.

   a Volleyball   b Snowboarding   c Rollerblading

4 We played tennis _____ .

   a yesterday afternoon   b last afternoon
   c afternoon ago

5 Luke and Kevin _____ a big argument on Friday.

   a had   b did   c said

6 I _____ the music was awesome!

   a taught   b thank   c thought

7 Your team _____ us in the championship.

   a beat   b win   c won

8 When _____ home?

   a she went   b did she go   c did she went

9 I _____ to Sarah on the phone.

   a didn't talk   b didn't talked   c wasn't talk

☐ 8

3 Vocabulary

Underline the correct words.

1 We went to the movies *last /
   ago / yesterday* night.

2 The movie started an hour *ago /
   last / now*.

3 It was my birthday *ago / last /
   two* week.

4 We arrived here *last / ago /
   yesterday* afternoon.

5 He's very tall, so he's good at
   swimming / basketball / cycling.

6 I love it when it snows. We can go
   skiing / swimming / surfing.

7 I only like team sports, so I don't
   like *skateboarding / volleyball /
   hockey*.

8 Always wear a *racket / helmet / stick*
   when you go cycling.

9 I love tennis, but our school doesn't
   have a *field / rink / court* where we
   can play.

☐ 8

How did you do?

Total: ☐ 25

| ☺ | Very good 25 – 20 | ☹ | OK 19 – 16 | ☹ | Review Unit 6 again 15 or less |

7 Successful people

1 Grammar

⁕ have to / don't have to

a Match the two parts of the sentences. Then match them with the pictures.
Write numbers 1–6 in the boxes.

1 Before our test, we
2 Jane can't go out now because she
3 To send a text message, you
4 I want a sandwich, so I
5 To drive a car, he
6 At Park School, every student

a has to get a driver's license.
b have to buy some bread.
c has to wear a uniform.
d have to study a lot.
e has to clean her room.
f have to use a cell phone.

b Put the words in order to make sentences.

1 my have I do school to after homework
   I have to do my homework after school.

2 at Doctors have good don't be to painting

   -- .

3 teacher everything A have know to doesn't

   -- .

4 do after have We the to lunch dishes

   -- .

5 You tomorrow have get up to don't early

   -- .

6 Roberto work the doesn't vacation have during to

   -- .

c Complete the sentences with *have/has to* or *don't/doesn't have to*.

1 A singer ___doesn't have to___ know how to swim.

2 Soccer players _____ be in really good shape.

3 A biology teacher _____ be good at science.

4 When you play tennis, you _____ run quickly.

5 A writer _____ be beautiful.

6 Waiters _____ go to college.

d Read the questions, look at the pictures and write the short answers.

1 Does Jeremy have to work at home?

Yes, he does.

2 Do Tom and Angela have to get up early?

_____ .

3 Does Jeremy have to do the grocery shopping?

_____ .

4 Does Angela have to cook breakfast?

_____ .

5 Does Angela have to iron the clothes?

_____ .

6 Do Jeremy's friends have to clean the swimming pool?

_____ .

e Look at the table. In the last row, check (✓) the things you have to do.
Then write questions with *have to* and short answers.

1 Mario  ?

A: *Does Mario have to cook?*

B: *Yes, he does.*

2 Giovanna and Stefano ?

A: _____ ?

B: _____ .

3 Giovanna ?

A: _____ ?

B: _____ .

4 Helena and Stefano  ?

A: _____ ?

B: _____ .

Mario		✓		✓
Giovanna	✓		✓	
Helena	✓	✓		
Stefano	✓			
YOU				

5 You ?

A: *Do you have to cook?*

B: *Yes, I do / No, I don't.*

6 You ?

A: _____ ?

B: _____ .

2 Vocabulary

✳ Jobs

a Find and (circle) the names of 12 jobs in the puzzle (→ or ↓).

b Write the jobs. Use ten words from the puzzle.

1 This person works in a school. _teacher_

2 These two people work on planes.

   .... + ...

3 These two people work in hospitals.

   .... + ...

4 This person puts fires out. ....

5 This person works with animals.

   ....

6 This person helps to make roads and bridges.

   ....

7 This person designs houses and buildings.

   ....

8 This person has to look inside people's mouths.

   ....

F	G	L	P	I	L	O	T	X	R	F	I	N
L	O	S	R	E	P	S	S	E	N	I	I	U
I	E	A	R	C	H	I	T	E	C	T	X	R
G	D	L	I	L	X	N	I	B	S	M	E	S
H	E	A	K	P	I	J	S	S	R	Y	F	E
T	N	W	Z	S	H	C	E	O	E	T	I	L
A	T	Y	Q	I	J	T	V	E	T	P	R	U
T	I	E	L	N	D	E	R	E	S	R	E	F
T	S	R	E	G	N	A	L	D	F	D	F	O
E	T	U	L	E	T	C	J	O	R	D	I	S
N	I	K	A	R	G	H	D	A	C	B	G	R
D	L	Y	T	I	O	E	Y	H	P	D	H	M
A	T	L	I	L	M	R	V	Q	S	X	T	A
N	I	O	P	I	D	O	C	T	O	R	E	E
T	J	E	N	G	I	N	E	E	R	H	R	B

c [Vocabulary bank] Complete the text with the words in the box.

in a store	salary	~~at home~~	in an office	wage	in a factory	night shift	earns

My dad doesn't leave the house for work. He works _at home_ . My mother works
¹ .... She sells things for computers.

My sister's a lawyer, so she works
² .... Her
³ .... is really good. She earns $80,000 a year.

My brother works ⁴ ....
It makes food for animals. He does a
⁵ .... from ten p.m. until eight in the morning.
His hourly ⁶ .... isn't very good. He only ⁷ .... $10 an hour, so he's looking for another job.

3 Pronunciation

✱ *have to*

a ▶ **CD3 T29** Listen and repeat.

1 We have to leave now.
2 They don't have to go out.
3 She has to do the laundry.
4 He doesn't have to study tonight.
5 Do you have to cook this evening?
6 Does he have to drive to the store?

b ▶ **CD3 T30** Listen and check (✓) the verb you hear: *have to, has to* or *had to*.

	have to	has to	had to
1		✓	
2			
3			
4			
5			
6			

4 Culture in mind

a Put the letters in the correct order to make words. Write them in the correct places.

krow lennio   imnwgo slnwa   ligerdvein swanppeers   ogd lawnkig   ~~tanigbysitb~~

1 _babysitting_   2 _____   3 _____   4 _____   5 _____

b Match the words and phrases in the box with the definitions.

> spending money   ~~customer~~
> to waste   to save
> to earn   to spend

1 someone who buys something (in a store) _customer_
2 to get money for doing a job _____
3 extra money to buy what you want _____
4 to put money in a bank _____
5 to use money to buy things _____
6 a bad use of money _____

5 Study help

✱ Vocabulary

Instead of putting new words in lists in your Vocabulary notebook, you can make a *word web*.

- Start with a topic word in a circle in the middle of the page.
- Write words connected to the topic word and then other words connected to those words, until you have a "web" of related words. Your word web can be as big as you like.
- There is no "correct" form for a word web. You choose the words and the way you organize them.

Here is a word web about *Jobs*. Write words in the empty circles. Then add more circles with words.

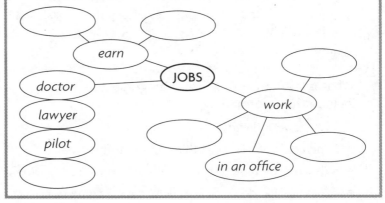

6 Read

These people all had dreams when they were young. Life wasn't easy for them, but they were determined, and they never gave up.

Match the two parts of the sentences. Then match the sentences with the photos. Write the numbers 1–5 in the boxes.

Frida Kahlo

Charles Dickens

Claudia Schiffer

Beethoven

Harrison Ford

1 He didn't show his writing to anyone because he thought it wasn't good,

2 When she was young, she only had one art class,

3 At school, she wasn't popular. No one thought she was good-looking,

4 His music teacher said he wasn't good enough to write music,

5 At school, he was nervous, and girls weren't interested in him,

a but she became a famous top model.

b but he became a great composer.

c but she became a famous painter.

d but he became a popular movie star.

e but he became a great writer.

7 Write

a Read the paragraph about Melanie's dream and what she has to do to make it come true. Fill in the blanks with words from Unit 7.

I really love information technology, and my dream is to be a _computer programmer_ with a company that makes software. I first started thinking about this three years ago. But it isn't going to be easy. I have to get some money to buy books and later to go to college. I don't get any ¹ _____ from my parents, because my mother doesn't have a ² _____, and my father doesn't ³ _____ a good salary. But now I'm delivering ⁴ _____ to get some money to buy the books. And on the weekend, I ⁵ _____ for our neighbors' young children.

b What is your dream? Write a paragraph about it. Include this information:

- What is your dream?
- When did you first start thinking about this dream?
- What do you have to do to make your dream come true?
- What are you doing now to help make it come true?

WRITING TIP

In your writing, it is useful to use connectors like *and*, *but* and *because* to link your ideas. Look at these three connectors in Exercises 6 and 7a. Then match the words with the definitions.

1 and   a links an event with a reason *why*

2 but   b links two ideas or events that are similar

3 because   c links two ideas or events that are different

Try to use each of these connectors in your paragraph for Exercise 7b.

Unit check

1 Fill in the blanks

Complete the text with the words in the box.

have   has   player   job   successful   doctors   dentist   dream   hours   ~~vet~~

Sonia's mother is a ___vet___ , her father is a [1] _____ and her two brothers are studying to be
[2] _____ . But Sonia isn't interested in getting a [3] _____ in medicine. She wants to become a
professional tennis [4] _____ , and her [5] _____ is to play tennis for her country at the Olympic
Games. Right now, she's on the girls' under-18 national team. Top tennis players [6] _____ to be in really
good shape, so every morning, Sonia gets up at 5:30 and runs for an hour before breakfast. Before and
after school, she goes to her tennis club because she has to practice for three [7] _____ a day. But she
also [8] _____ to go to school and do her homework in the evening. It's very hard work, but Sonia is
determined to be [9] _____ in her sport.

9

2 Choose the correct answers

Circle the correct answer: a, b or c.

1 _____ help people when they are in the hospital.

   a (Nurses) b Vets c Dentists

2 _____ fly planes.

   a Pilots b Lawyers c Drivers

3 Computer _____ put information into computers.

   a attendants b programmers c players

4 I took my dog to the _____ because he was sick.

   a vet b engineer c firefighter

5 To be a lawyer, you have to get very good _____
   in school.

   a exams b dreams c grades

6 John _____ money in the bank to buy
   a good computer.

   a saves b earns c works

7 You're lucky! You _____ do the dishes.

   a have to b has to c don't have to

8 A pop singer _____ have to go to college.

   a doesn't b don't c didn't

9 We don't have much time, so we _____
   be quick.

   a have to b has to c don't have to

8

3 Vocabulary

Underline the word that doesn't fit in each group.

1 cooking   ironing   <u>running</u>   cleaning
2 babysitting   dog-walking   part-time   mowing lawns
3 earn   vet   engineer   architect
4 teacher   pilot   lawyer   job
5 doctor   nurse   pilot   vet
6 wages   full-time   salary   spending money

7 dentist   teacher   nurse   doctor
8 earn   spend   save   work
9 office   home   factory   store

8

How did you do?

Total: **25**

😊	Very good 25 – 20	😐	OK 19 – 16	☹	Review Unit 7 again 15 or less

8 Eat for life.

1 Remember and check

Complete the sentences with the words in the box. Then check with the text on page 50 of the Student's Book.

> bad   different   green   healthy   ~~long~~   stress-free

1 The women of Okinawa live a _long_ time.

2 They have a very .... diet.

3 They eat fish, fruit and .... vegetables.

4 Seaweed has many .... vitamins and minerals.

5 The fat in sweets, fried food and meat is .... for us.

6 It is good to live a .... life, if possible.

2 Vocabulary

✽ Food and drink

a Fill in the crossword.

Across →	Down ↓
1 	1 
4 	2 
6 	3 
9 	5 
	7 
	8 

b Use some of the crossword answers to complete the sentences.

1 .....Oranges..... grow on trees.

2 .... and .... grow under the ground.

3 .... and .... have milk in them.

4 You can drink ....

5 You use .... in an omelette.

6 .... makes your coffee sweet.

c Put the letters in the correct order to label the food and drinks in the picture.

seprag   fefcoe   klim   ~~edrab~~   meotosta   insoon

1   *bread*
2
3
4
5   6

3 Grammar

✳ Count and noncount nouns

a Are the words in Exercises 2a and 2c count or noncount nouns? Write them in the correct lists.

Count	Noncount
grapes	*coffee*

✳ *a/an* and *some*

b Underline the correct verb in each sentence.

1   There *is* / *are* some fruit on the table.
2   There *is* / *are* some meat in the fridge.
3   There *is* / *are* some sandwiches in the kitchen.
4   There *is* / *are* some money in my bag.
5   There *is* / *are* some paper in the box.
6   There *is* / *are* some pens on Brian's desk.
7   There *is* / *are* some information about the city in this book.
8   There *is* / *are* some good songs on this CD.

c Complete the sentences with *a*, *an* or *some*.

1   We need _some_ yogurt, _some_ juice and _some_ eggs.
2   For lunch, she's having .... apple and .... cheese.
3   I want to make a sandwich. I need .... tomato and .... bread.
4   The boys are hungry, but there's only .... orange and .... tomatoes in the kitchen.
5   Let's buy .... mineral water and .... vegetable soup at the supermarket.
6   Can I have .... oranges, please? I want to make .... orange juice.
7   John's in the kitchen. He's drinking .... cup of coffee and eating .... ice cream.
8   You can't make pasta. You only have .... carrot and .... onions!

d Write four sentences about the things that are on your desk. Use *There is/are* with *a*, *an* or *some*.

There are some pens and some pencils on my desk.

....
....
....
....

✱ much and many

e Complete the dialogue with the words in the box.

much sugar	many hours	much exercise
many emails	~~much food~~	many calories
much weight		

Denise: What do you want to eat?

Sarah: Just a sandwich, I think. I don't eat __much food__ at lunchtime. How ¹ _____ are there in this drink?

Denise: I don't know, but I don't think there's ² _____ in it.

Sarah: I would rather have some water. I'm on a diet, but I'm not losing ³ _____ .

Denise: That's because you don't get ⁴ _____ . Stop worrying about your food and try to get in shape. How ⁵ _____ a week do you spend sitting in front of the computer?

Sarah: A lot! But I can't help it. Do you know how ⁶ _____ I get? About 50 every day. I spend two hours answering them every afternoon!

f Fill in the blanks with *much* or *many*.

I go to a great school! We don't have __many__ classes – only four a day. In the classes, we don't do ¹ _____ reading. The activities are usually speaking and listening to music. There aren't ² _____ teachers, and they're all really cool! They never give us ³ _____ homework. We get one or two short exercises a week. We don't have ⁴ _____ tests, and they're always very easy, so we don't spend ⁵ _____ time studying.

Of course, there isn't ⁶ _____ truth to this! I don't think there's a school like that, but it's fun to imagine it!

4 Vocabulary

a **Vocabulary bank** Find eight more things we use to eat or drink in the wordsnake and (circle) them.

cupspoonforkstrawknife(plate)glassbowlsaucer

b Use the words from Exercise 4a to label the picture.

1 __plate__   2 _____

3 _____   4 _____

5 _____   6 _____

7 _____   8 _____

9 _____

5 Pronunciation

✱ The schwa /ə/ (the)

a ▶ **CD3 T31** Listen and <u>underline</u> the main stress in each phrase. Then circle the syllables with the /ə/ sound.

1 wa(ter) with lem(on)
2 bacon and eggs
3 bananas and apples
4 some fruit and vegetables
5 a healthy breakfast
6 a good diet

b ▶ **CD3 T32** Complete the phrases with words from Exercise 5a. Then listen, check and repeat.

Jenny has _bacon_ and eggs. Terrance
has [1] .... and butter. Ollie
has [2] .... and apples. Fruit
is important in a good [3] ....
It's important to eat [4] .... ,
too. A healthy [5] .... is good
for you, but you should also exercise.

6 Everyday English

Complete the expressions.

1 A: Samantha? Can you come over to my place and help me with something?

   B: Sure, n<u>o</u> p<u>roblem</u> ! I'll be there in a [1] c............ o............ minutes, OK?

2 A: My parents want me to help out at home. You know, take the trash out, clean my room [2] a............ s............ . It's boring, right?

   B: Yeah, I [3] k............ w............ y............ m............ ! I have to do the dishes every night!

3 A: Do you enjoy running?

   B: [4] A............ ! It's a lot of fun. It's better in the rain [5] a............ w............ !

7 Study help

✱ Vocabulary

Adjectives often have either a positive or a negative meaning. You can group them under these two headings in your Vocabulary notebook.

Look at these adjectives. Write them in the correct lists.

Then add two more adjectives to each list.

> ~~awful~~ unhealthy ~~fantastic~~ delicious
> difficult successful sick interesting
> healthy great boring beautiful
> crazy unhappy

Positive adjectives	Negative adjectives
fantastic	_awful_
....	....
....	....
....	....
....	....
....	....
....	....
....	....

8 Read

a In this text, three people are describing their favorite meal. Read the text and answer the questions.

1 Who doesn't eat meat? ....*Maria*........

2 Who doesn't have cheese in their meal? ....

3 Who has some bread with their meal? ....

4 Who uses tomatoes in their meal? ....

b Complete the table with words from the text.

Meat	Fruit and vegetables	Other food
beef		

Favorite food

Diane: My favorite food is lasagne. I make it with beef or sausage in a delicious sauce. Of course, you need pasta as well, and some tomatoes for the sauce. I put lots of cheese in my lasagne, and I usually eat it with a green salad.

Diane

Max: I really love Indian curries. My dad often makes curry using chicken or beef and onions and yogurt. We have it with rice. Some people have Indian bread with their curry, but I don't like it very much.

Max

Maria: I'm a vegetarian, and one of my favorite dishes is carrot soup. It's very good for you, and it's quick and easy to make. You just need carrots, onions and potatoes and juice from an orange. When I serve the soup, I put cheese on top, and I eat it with bread.

Maria

READING TIP

Reading for specific information

Question 8a tells you the general idea of the text and asks you to find specific information.

- First read the questions carefully. Notice the question word *Who ... ?* This tells you that each answer will be a person. Check the text quickly to find the people's names.

- <u>Underline</u> key words in the question (for example, *Who doesn't eat <u>meat</u>?*) When you read, look for the key words (for example, *meat*) and for related words (for example, *beef, chicken*). Focus on these parts of the text and read them carefully.

- Look out for negatives in the questions and in the text. These are important for the meaning, and they are sometimes a little difficult!

9 Write

Choose some of the food in the picture, and write about a dish that you like.

Unit check

1 Fill in the blanks

Complete the text with the words in the box.

> fish   apple   doesn't   some   breakfast   vegetables   ~~food~~   eats   beef   oranges

Cooking is a problem in the Linton family because everyone wants different _food_ . Mr. Linton likes
[1] _____ meat in every meal. He has eggs and sausage for [2] _____ , and his favorite dish is roast
[3] _____ . Mrs. Linton doesn't like red meat, so she only eats chicken and [4] _____ . Their son Chris
is a vegetarian. This means that he [5] _____ eat meat at all. For lunch, he usually has a salad, and in the
evening, he has [6] _____ with pasta or rice. He also [7] _____ a lot of fruit. He has an [8] _____
or some [9] _____ every day. So when the Lintons sit down for dinner, there are often three different
meals on the table.

☐ 9

2 Choose the correct answers

(Circle) the correct answer: a, b or c.

1 Are you ready to _____ ?

   a (order) b food c drink

2 _____ are my favorite vegetables.

   a Eggs b Bananas c Carrots

3 A: I'd like some fruit.

   B: OK. There are some _____ in the kitchen.

   a potatoes b apples c rice

4 We need to buy some _____ .

   a onions b orange c tomato

5 She doesn't have _____ bread.

   a a b much c lot of

6 Would you like _____ cheese sandwich?

   a some b a c an

7 There _____ sugar in my coffee.

   a isn't much b aren't many c aren't much

8 You need _____ onions for this soup.

   a a lot b lots c a lot of

9 I want to buy _____ at the store.

   a a milk b some milk c some milks

☐ 8

3 Vocabulary

What are they? Write:

F (= Fruit)   V (= Vegetable)   O (= Other food)   D (= Drink)   T (= Things we use to eat/drink)

1	onion	_V_	7	knife	_____	13	orange juice _____
2	sugar	_O_	8	banana	_____	14	orange _____
3	straw	_____	9	milk	_____	15	lemon _____
4	bread	_____	10	fork	_____	16	plate _____
5	apple	_____	11	water	_____	17	potato chips _____
6	eggs	_____	12	cheese	_____	18	glass _____

☐ 16

How did you do?

Total: ☐ 33

😊	Very good 33 – 26	😐	OK 25 – 22	☹	Review Unit 8 again 21 or less

9 Learning Languages

1 Remember and check

Think back to the text about Giuseppe Mezzofanti. Can you match 1–6 with their definitions a–f? Check your answers with the text on page 58 of the Student's Book.

1	38	a	the number of months he took to learn Chinese
2	1	b	the number of languages he could understand (but not speak)
3	12	c	the number of languages he spoke fluently
4	4	d	the number of countries he lived in or visited
5	20	e	the number of prisoners he went to speak to in a new language
6	2	f	the age at which he could speak about nine languages

2 Grammar

✳ Comparative adjectives

a Read what Sarah says about her mother. Find 11 adjectives and underline them.

> My mother is studying Russian in her <u>free</u> time. She goes to a small class at our local college, and she practices conversation with an old friend, who is an excellent teacher. The Russian alphabet is different from our alphabet, and that was strange at first. But Mom is good at languages, and she's very determined. She's planning a big vacation to Russia and Poland soon, and I think that's a really exciting idea.

b Write the adjectives and their comparative forms in the table.

exciting good small quiet big easy difficult bad expensive successful cheap noisy far relaxing old

-er	more ...	irregular
small – smaller	exciting – more exciting	good – better

c Compare the two cafés. Write sentences with some of the adjectives from Exercise 2b.

1 *Café Paradiso is smaller than Efes Café.*
2 _____ .
3 _____ .
4 _____ .
5 _____ .
6 _____ .

EFES CAFÉ

Our famous coffee –
just $1.40

A range of
sandwiches at $4.50

Big game room
with video screen
and five pool tables

Café Paradiso

Just opened!!

Coffee $1.25
Fresh sandwiches
from only $3.25

small but friendly,
relaxing atmosphere

3 Vocabulary

✱ Language learning

a Match the words and phrases to make expressions about language learning.

1	have	a	the meaning of a word
2	imitate	b	in a dictionary
3	make	c	other speakers
4	guess	d	mistakes
5	look up a word	e	an accent
6	translate from	f	mistake
7	correct a	g	a word means
8	know what	h	your first language

b Complete the text with verbs from Exercise 3a.

If you don't ___know___ what a word means, try
to ¹ _____ the meaning, or
² _____ the word in your dictionary.

All learners ³ _____ an accent, but
that doesn't matter. To make your pronunciation
better, listen to English speakers and try to
⁴ _____ them. Don't worry if you
⁵ _____ mistakes. It's normal!

It's sometimes useful to ⁶ _____
words from one language to the other, but it's
better if you try to think in the new language.

c Complete the sentences with the words in the box.

> foreign   fluently   native speaker
> official language   communicate
> accuracy   ~~native language~~   .

1 He lives in Australia, but his
  native language isn't English. It's Greek!
2 He's from the U.S., so he's a
  _____ of English. But he also
  speaks three _____ languages.
3 He speaks easily and quickly. He speaks
  Chinese _____ .
4 Portuguese is the _____ of
  Brazil.
5 His _____ is good. He almost
  never makes grammar mistakes!
6 I'm studying Russian so I can
  _____ with my host family in
  Moscow next summer.

4 Grammar

✱ Superlative adjectives

a Write the adjectives and their superlative forms in the boxes.

> ~~high~~ ~~boring~~ beautiful bad big
> important easy good thin
> delicious heavy creative short
> rich intelligent

-est	irregular
high – the highest	_____
_____	_____
_____	
_____	
_____	
_____	

most ...
boring – the most boring
_____
_____
_____
_____

b Complete the sentences. Use superlative adjectives from Exercise 4a.

1 This is the ____heaviest____ bag in the world! What do you have in it?

2 London is about 1,580 square km. It's one of the _____ cities in Europe.

3 That was the _____ soccer game ever! I almost fell asleep.

4 Marilyn Monroe was one of the _____ women in Hollywood in the 1950s.

5 I don't have any problems with math. For me, it's the _____ subject at school.

6 Mr. Thomas has four cars and an amazing house near the beach. He's the _____ person in our town.

7 All the food is good here, but the fish soup is the _____ thing on the menu.

✳ Comparative or superlative?

c Read Paula's email to her friend Rafael in Mexico. Write the correct forms of the adjectives in parentheses. Add any other necessary words.

Hi, Rafael!

I'm writing this from San Francisco! We got here on Tuesday, after staying in San Diego and Los Angeles. San Francisco is one of the __most interesting__ (interesting) cities in California, but unfortunately, it's also one of [1] _____ (expensive) places to stay. It's [2] _____ (small) Los Angeles and Mexico City, so it's easy to walk around. We did a lot of shopping. I think Union Square has [3] _____ (good) places to shop in the city! It's [4] _____ (difficult) to communicate with people here than it was in San Diego because more people speak Spanish in San Diego. But that's OK. The people are [5] _____ (friendly) here, and I need to practice English!

I ate [6] _____ (delicious) food in my life here in Chinatown. I think Chinese food is the [7] _____ (good) food in America. Tomorrow we're going to the "Mission." It's [8] _____ (old) part of the city. There is a restaurant there that is famous for burritos. My aunt, who is American, said they are [9] _____ (bigger) the burritos in Mexico. Maybe...but I don't think they'll taste as good!

We're flying home to Mexico City in five days. See you then!

Paula

d Write one comparative and one superlative sentence about the things in each group. Use your own ideas.

football – tennis – volleyball

Football is more exciting than tennis. Volleyball is the easiest sport.

1 New York – Rome – Rio de Janeiro

....

....

2 winter – spring – summer

....

....

3 rock music – rap music – classical music

....

....

4 English – French – Japanese

....

....

5 Pronunciation

✳ Sentence stress

a ▶ **CD3 T33** Listen to the sentences and <u>underline</u> the stressed syllables.

1 <u>Cars</u> are <u>fast</u>er (than) <u>bic</u>y(cles).

2 Chocolate is sweeter than butter.

3 Paula is more creative than her brother.

4 Robert is the youngest student in our class.

5 Vegetables are healthy.

6 It was the most expensive jacket in the store.

b ▶ **CD3 T33** Listen again and (circle) the syllables with the /ə/ sound. Then listen, check and repeat.

6 Culture in mind

Complete the summary of the text. Use the words in the box.

> sweet   groovy   ~~invent~~   expressions   rents
> decades   group   hang out   creative

Teenagers never like to be the same as their parents, so they often _____invent_____ their own "language." When teenagers ¹ _____ with each other and talk, they use words and
² _____ that older people don't always understand.

This "teen talk" changes all the time. In the United States, there were different words for *good* in different ³ _____ .
For example, in the 1960s, people often said ⁴ " _____ ," and in the 1990s a word for *good* was ⁵ " _____ ."

Perhaps the strongest reason for "teen talk" is that teenagers want to be part of a ⁶ _____ that is different and special. Another reason is that teenagers are very ⁷ _____ with language. But they also like it when older people, like their ⁸ " _____ ," don't always understand them!

7 Study help

✳ Self-assessment

Answer these questions. Think about your progress as a language learner.

1 Why is English important in your country? Give three reasons.

_____

_____

_____

2 How can English help you in the future? Write three ideas.

_____

_____

_____

3 What do you know in English now that you didn't know a year ago? Write three things.

_____

_____

_____

4 Check (✓) the correct box for you.

	In English ...	I'm really good at this	I'm OK at this	I'm not very good at this
a	grammar			
b	vocabulary			
c	reading			
d	writing			
e	listening			
f	speaking			

8 Listen

a ▶ CD3 T34 Listen to Sergio talking about his sisters, Maria, Julia, Lara and Ana. Match the people in the pictures with their names and with the things they own.

Sergio   Maria   Julia   Lara   Ana

GIRLS AROUND

ALL MY LOVE TERRY x

b ▶ CD3 T34 Listen again. Write *T* (true) or *F* (false).

1 Maria was born before the other girls. `T`

2 Sergio doesn't like Maria's hair. ☐

3 Julia is an intelligent girl. ☐

4 Julia is funnier than Maria. ☐

5 Lara and Ana often argue about animals. ☐

6 Lara is good at swimming. ☐

9 Write

Choose one of these topics:

● three members of your family

● three singers/groups

● three athletes

● three TV/movie stars who are popular in your country

Write a paragraph to compare the three people you chose. Use comparative and superlative adjectives.

LISTENING TIP

Here's an idea for practicing listening outside the classroom. Work with a friend. Every week, prepare a message in English and record it. Exchange recordings and listen to your friend's message. The topic of your message can be anything that interests you.

If you have a way of making a recording at home, you can start now. Use Sergio's recording as an example and describe the people in your family.

Other ideas for listening practice outside the class:

● Listen to English speakers and try to hear what they are saying.

● Listen to radio shows in English on the Internet. For example, listen to some of the NPR (National Public Radio) programs.

● Watch movies/videos in English with subtitles. Turn off the subtitles as you watch and try to understand the dialogue.

● Listen to songs in English. If you want to read the words while you listen, you can probably find them on the Internet.

Unit check

1 Fill in the blanks

Complete the text with the words in the box.

> easier   guess   speak   ~~went~~   accent   worst   than   imitate   difficult   look

Michelle and Luc were born in France, but their family _went_ to live in Verona two years ago, and now they both [1] _____ Italian. Michelle is older [2] _____ her brother, and at first she found the new language more [3] _____ to learn. "I think it's [4] _____ to pick up a language when you're younger," she said. For her, pronunciation is the [5] _____ problem. "A lot of Italian vocabulary is similar to French, so I can often [6] _____ the meaning of words. I don't have to [7] _____ them up in a dictionary," she said. "But I still have a strong French [8] _____ , and sometimes people find it difficult to understand me. As soon as Luc went to school, he began to [9] _____ the other children, and he speaks almost perfect Italian now."

> 9

2 Choose the correct answers

(Circle) the correct answer: a, b or c.

1 Jessie _____ four languages.

   a (speaks)   b says   c tells

2 I don't want to _____ any mistakes on my math test.

   a do   b make   c get

3 They're _____ a book from German into English.

   a correcting   b translating   c communicating

4 Look _____ these words in your dictionary.

   a up   b down   c to

5 Young children usually _____ their parents.

   a communicate   b imitate   c guess

6 He's one of the _____ movie stars in the world.

   a most successful   b successfuller   c successfullest

7 Britney is _____ than the other students in the class.

   a tall   b taller   c the tallest

8 Mrs. Wilson is the _____ person on our street.

   a more friendly   b friendliest   c more friendliest

9 All the food was great, but the soup was _____ .

   a the better   b the most good   c the best

> 8

3 Vocabulary

Underline the correct words.

1 My mother's from Switzerland. She's a _native_ / accuracy speaker of German.

2 They're from Japan, so they have a Japanese sound / accent when they speak English.

3 Our teacher always corrects / mistakes us when we get something wrong.

4 If you don't know what the word means / says, use a dictionary!

5 I didn't know the answer, so I had to translate / guess.

6 English is my first language, so Spanish is a regional / foreign language for me.

7 You didn't answer the questions very accurately / creatively. Please study more for the next test.

8 My dad says the 1990s were the best years / decade of his life.

9 "Cool!" is my favorite expression / communication in English.

> 8

How did you do?

Total: [ ] 25

|  Very good 25 – 20 |  OK 19 – 16 | 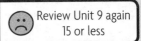 Review Unit 9 again 15 or less |

1 Remember and check

<u>Underline</u> the correct words. Then check with Exercise 1c on page 65 of the Student's Book.

1 Anna and her *father / mother* are planning a family vacation.
2 They're going to Costa Rica in *April / May*.
3 They're going by *train / plane* to San José.
4 They're staying in *San José / Talamanca*.
5 They're going to help *sea turtles / fish*.
6 Anna's dad almost *laughed / fainted* when he heard how much the trip cost.

2 Grammar

⭑ Present continuous for future arrangements

a Complete the text about Maggie's vacation plans. Use the present continuous form of the verb in parentheses.

Maggie __isn't staying__ (not stay) home next summer. She ¹ _____ (take) a vacation in Mazatlán with her family. Her parents ² _____ (pay) for the vacation, and Maggie's brother Steve ³ _____ (go), too. They ⁴ _____ (not fly) to Mexico. They ⁵ _____ (drive) from San Diego to Baja California. From there, they ⁶ _____ (travel) by ferry to Mazatlán. Maggie said, "I ⁷ _____ (not spend) a lot of time at the beach this year because Steve doesn't want to do that. But we ⁸ _____ (hike) a lot. I'm really looking forward to it."

b Alan wants to invite Marta to his house one afternoon next week, but which day? Look at Marta's calendar and write her replies.

Mon
Helen coming to my place

Tues
Go shopping with Dad

Wed
Study for math test

Thurs
Play tennis with Jane

Fri
4:30 Meet Uncle Jack at airport

Sat
Have lunch with Grandma

Sun
Cousins arriving from Brazil

1 Thursday? — *Sorry, I'm playing tennis with Jane on Thursday.*

2 Saturday? _____

3 Friday? _____

4 Sunday? _____

5 Monday? _____

6 Wednesday? _____

7 Tuesday? _____

c Complete the dialogues with questions and short answers.
Use the present continuous form of the verbs in parentheses.

Michael: It's my birthday next Friday.

Kristin: That's nice. _Are you having_ (you / have) a party?

Michael: Yes, _I am_ . And I want you to come.

Kristin: Great! Thanks, Michael.
¹ .... (Tyler / come)?

Michael: No, ² .... He's working on Friday.

Kristin: Oh, I see. ³ .... (Anna and Liam / come)?

Michael: Yes, ⁴ ....

Kristin: Oh, good!

Justin: ⁵ .... (you and your family / go) on vacation this year?

Savannah: Yes, ⁶ .... We're visiting my aunt in Puerto Rico in July.

Justin: Great! ⁷ .... (you / travel) by boat?

Savannah: No, ⁸ .... We're going by plane.

Justin: ⁹ .... (your sister / go) with you?

Savannah: Yes, ¹⁰ ....

✱ Present continuous: now or in the future?

d Look at the underlined verbs. Are they about now or about the future? Write *N* (now) or *F* (future).

Jenny: Hello, this is Jenny.

Mason: Hi, Jenny. It's Mason. What <u>are</u> you <u>doing</u> (_N_)?

Jenny: Hi, Mason. Oh, not too much.
We<u>'re having</u> (¹ ....) dinner in a few minutes.
What about you?

Mason: Me? I<u>'m watching</u> (² ....) soccer on TV. It isn't a very good game.

Jenny: Yeah? Who<u>'s winning</u>? (³ ....)

Mason: The Galaxy, 3–0. But listen, Jenny, what <u>are</u> you <u>doing</u> (⁴ ....) on Saturday?

Jenny: Saturday? I<u>'m not doing</u> (⁵ ....) anything. Why?

Mason: Well, Adam and I <u>are meeting</u> (⁶ ....) at the beach. Do you want to come?

Jenny: Yes, OK.

Mason: Great. We<u>'re planning</u> (⁷ ....) to have lunch there at about one o'clock.

Jenny: OK. My mom and I <u>are going</u> (⁸ ....) grocery shopping in the morning. I can buy some food and bring it with me.

Mason: Excellent!

Jenny: Look, I can't talk any more now. Dad<u>'s calling</u> (⁹ ....) me. But I'll see you on Saturday, OK?

Mason: OK, great. See you then.

3 Vocabulary

✱ Future time expressions

a Replace the underlined words with time expressions from the box.

1 It's June now. Vacation is beginning <u>in July</u>.
   next month

2 Today is Wednesday. I'm going to the dentist <u>on Friday</u>.
   ....

3 It's four o'clock now. The show is starting <u>at seven o'clock</u>.
   ....

next week/month/year	the day after tomorrow
the week/month/year after next	

in [number]	hours
	days
	weeks
	months
	years

4 It's 2010 now. We're buying a new car <u>in 2011</u>.
   ....

5 It's Saturday, May 4 today. Brian is playing basketball <u>on Saturday May 25</u>.
   ....

✳ Vacation activities

b Fill in the crossword.

(crossword) SIGHTSEEING

c Write the words in the lists to make expressions for talking about vacation activities.

> by plane   a boat   at home   a week   ~~souvenirs~~
> a postcard   on a farm   a car   some time
> to Boston   by car   three days   presents
> canoes   in a hotel

stay ...	travel ...	rent ...
....	....	....
....	....	....
....	....	....

spend ...	buy ...
....	*souvenirs*
....	....
....	....

d Complete the sentences with expressions from Exercise 3c.

1   I'd like to _buy_ some _souvenirs_ . I want to remember this place!

2   They were away for a week. They _____ in Greece and four days in Germany.

3   We _____ at the airport and drove around Ireland.

4   A: How did you get to Prague?
    B: I _____ . There was a flight at three o'clock.

5   A: Did you go camping in France?
    B: No, we _____ in Paris.

e **Vocabulary bank** Complete the text with the words in the box.

> buy   go   learn   looking   meet
> ~~take~~   try   visiting

from: alima55@aeim.cup

I'm really excited because next weekend we're going on a school trip to Paris! Of course, I'm planning to _take_ a lot of photographs, and I want to [1] _____ to speak French, too. I think we're [2] _____ all of the famous monuments and maybe going on a trip on the Seine River and [3] _____ at those famous views! I want to [4] _____ some souvenirs to take home for my family, too. We're not staying for very long – only three days – but maybe I can [5] _____ some local people and [6] _____ about local customs. I want to [7] _____ to a market, too – the one on Rue Mouffetard.

4 Pronunciation

✱ /θ/ (_think_) and /ð/ (_that_)

a ▶CD3 T35 How do you say _th_ in these words? Write them in the correct lists. Then listen, check and repeat.

> them   those   math   father   thousand   thirteen   athlete   throw   brother   these

/θ/ (_think_)   ....

/ð/ (_that_)   ....

b ▶CD3 T36 Listen and repeat.

1   It's my 16th birthday next month.
2   They're sunbathing together on the beach.
3   Her grandfather is healthy, but he's very thin.
4   My brother can throw this ball farther than me.

5 Everyday English

Circle the correct words.

1   **A:** I don't have any money.

   B: That's OK. I don't have any money _then / either_!

2   **A:** I'm sure the test tomorrow is going to be really hard.

   B: Look, _don't worry / hang on_. It's not a very important test, OK?

3   **A:** I'm bored.

   B: Let's go out and do something, _either / then_!

4   **A:** Oh, no! We missed the bus!

   B: I know, but _it's your fault / hang on_. You had to stop and take pictures, not me.

5   **A:** Don't you know the answer?

   B: No, I'm sorry. I have no idea _then / at all_.

6   **A:** Let's go, Jimmy.

   B: _Wait a sec. / Don't worry_. I need to make a phone call. I'll be quick, OK?

6 Study help

✱ Using a dictionary (1)

a Here are some abbreviations (short forms) that you find in a dictionary. Can you figure out what the words are?

1   _n_   ____noun____   4   _prep_   ....
2   _v_   5   _sing_   ....
3   _adj_   6   _pl_   ....

b Look at the dictionary entry for _cancel_ and match the parts with the words in the box. Write letters a–e in the boxes.

a   the meaning of the word
b   an example using the word
c   the pronunciation
d   the part of speech (noun, verb, etc.)
e   the main stress

☐1   ☐2   ☐3   ☐4   ☐5

cancel /ˈkænsəl/ _v_ to decide that something that was arranged is not happening: _We're canceling tomorrow's soccer game because of bad weather_

c Read the entry for _reservation_.

reservation /rezərveɪʃən/ _n_ an arrangement for something like a seat on an aircraft or a table at a restaurant to be kept for you: _I'd like to make a reservation for two people for dinner at seven o'clock._

Circle the correct meaning for this sentence: _We canceled our hotel reservation._

1   We now have a room at the hotel.
2   We no longer have a room at the hotel.
3   We couldn't get a room at the hotel.

7 Read

Read Emma's email to Adam. Write the answers to the questions.

> Hi Adam!
>
> Guess what? Next week is my father's 50th birthday, and we're having a party on Saturday night. It's a secret! Dad doesn't know about it. My mom, my brother and I are organizing it. We're using a big room in a hotel in town, and we're bringing in flowers and putting up decorations on Saturday morning. We're hiring a jazz band to play music during the evening.
>
> My aunt and uncle are coming from Australia. They're arriving on Friday, and they're staying in the hotel because our apartment is very small. But my grandfather can't come because he's still in the hospital. I'm very sad about that.
>
> We're inviting all of Dad's friends. Mom's making a birthday cake, and she's hiring a catering company to serve the food and drinks. Tomorrow morning, she and I are going out to buy some new clothes to wear. I hope I can find something nice!
>
> I'll get in touch after the party and tell you all about it.
>
> Love,
> Emma

1 Who is 50 years old next week?
   Emma's father.

2 When and where are they having the party?
   ----

3 Who is coming from Australia?
   ----

4 When are they arriving?
   ----

5 Why aren't they staying at Emma's apartment?
   ----

6 Who can't come to the party? Why not?
   ----

7 What are Emma and her mother doing tomorrow?

READING TIP

Writing answers about a reading text

- First read the questions carefully and make sure you know what they are asking. <u>Underline</u> the question words to help you look for the right information.

- Follow the advice on reading for specific information on page 48.

- Questions starting with *Who, When* or *Where* usually only need short answers: a name, a time or a place. Questions starting with *Why* need a longer answer to give a reason for something.

8 Listen

▶ CD3 T37 Listen to the phone conversation between Emma and Adam after the party. Were the party arrangements successful? Write a ✓ if things were good and an ✗ if there was a problem.

Unit check

1 Fill in the blanks

Complete the text with the words in the box.

| aren't | is | breakfast | ~~vacation~~ | sunbathing | campsite | snorkeling | canoeing | plane | renting |

Next month, Rich and Kevin are going to Belize for their summer _vacation_ . They're traveling by
¹_____ to Belize City, and for the first four nights they're staying in a bed and ²_____ on the
coast. They like water sports, so they want to go ³_____ and windsurfing in the ocean. They also plan
to spend some time ⁴_____ on the beach. After that, they're taking a bus to San Ignacio. They're
⁵_____ bikes to ride around town and by the river. They're ⁶_____ on the river, too. They
⁷_____ taking much money with them, and they enjoy being outdoors. So, they're staying at a
⁸_____ near San Ignacio. They're flying back to Dallas on August 16, and Rich's father ⁹_____
meeting them at the airport.

| | 9 |

2 Choose the correct answers

(Circle) the correct answer: a, b or c.

1 Sandra went _____ on the river.

   a snorkeling   b (canoeing)   c horseback riding

2 You can rent _____ at the beach.

   a postcards   b hotels   c surfboards

3 We traveled from Italy to Greece _____ ferry.

   a on   b by   c with

4 Caroline and Mia are _____ three months in Africa.

   a spending   b saving   c camping

5 I need to buy a _____ for this letter.

   a souvenir   b stamp   c present

6 _____ working in the restaurant next weekend.

   a I not   b I'm not   c I don't

7 Where _____ for his next vacation?

   a he going   b he's going   c is he going

8 It's January now, so March is the month after _____ .

   a next   b today   c tomorrow

9 We're leaving for Australia in four _____ .

   a weekend   b months   c time

| | 8 |

3 Vocabulary

Write a word or phrase from the box beside
each picture. There are three extra words.

| ~~taking photographs~~   sailing   hiking |
| horseback riding   snorkeling |
| going to a market   buying souvenirs |
| climbing   sunbathing   camping |
| windsurfing   visiting monuments |

1   _taking photographs_

2   _____

3   _____

4   _____

5   _____

6   _____

7   _____

8   _____

9   _____

| | 8 |

How did you do?

Total: | 25 |

| 😊 | Very good 25 – 20 | 😐 | OK 19 – 16 | 😞 | Review Unit 10 again 15 or less |

11 It'll never happen.

1 Remember and check

Complete the predictions with the phrases in the box. Then check with the text on page 72 of the Student's Book.

> will never be able   has no   is on the way out   ~~would ever want~~   there is   won't last
> anyone would want   you're crazy

1. A U.S. president in 1872: "[The telephone is] an amazing invention, but who _would ever want_ to use one?"

2. A scientist in 1899: "Radio _____ future."

3. In the *New York Times* in 1936: "A rocket _____ to leave the earth's atmosphere."

4. The head of IBM in 1943: "I think _____ a world market for maybe five computers."

5. A movie producer in 1946: "Television _____ ."

6. Edwin Drake in 1859: "Drill for oil? _____ ."

7. A man at a record company in 1962: "We don't like their sound, and guitar music _____ ."

8. The head of DEC in 1977: "There is no reason _____ a computer in their home."

2 Grammar

✱ *will/won't*

a Match the sentences with the pictures. Write numbers 1–8 in the boxes.

1. Jim, come on! Hurry! We _will be_ late for school!

2. Don't worry about tomorrow's test. I'm sure it _____ very difficult.

3. They _____ today. There aren't any good players on the team.

4. I don't know how to fix this! I'll call Bob. I'm sure he _____ me.

5. Let's look on the Internet. Maybe we _____ some information there.

6. Please don't buy that dress for me, Mom. I _____ it.

7. Don't be scared. The dog _____ us.

8. Please sit down. The doctor _____ you soon.

b Complete the sentences in Exercise 2a. Use *will* or *won't* and the verbs in the box.

> help   ~~be~~   find   see   be   hurt   wear   win

c Read the answers and complete the questions.

1 A: _Will_ Liz and Sean _get_ married?

   B: Yes, I think they will. They really love each other.

2 A: _____ Chloe _____ to the party?

   B: Yes, of course she'll come.

3 A: _____ Jenny _____ to college when she finishes school?

   B: No, she won't. She wants to go to art school.

4 A: It's late! _____ your parents _____ angry?

   B: Well, they won't be very happy.

5 A: When _____ Chris _____ painting his room?

   B: I think he'll finish it tomorrow.

6 A: Where _____ you _____ Aaron?

   B: I think I'll see him at the gym on Friday.

d Matt is thinking about his future. Write his predictions.

1 _I will go to college_ , and _I'll become a vet._

2 _____ , but _____ .

3 _____ , but _____ .

4 _____ , but _____ .

e Complete the sentences with your own predictions. Use _'ll/will_ or _won't_.

1 In a few years, I _____ .

2 When I finish school, I _____ .

3 Before I'm 30, I _____ .

4 I think my best friend _____ .

5 In the future, my town _____ .

6 In 20 years, _____ .

3 Pronunciation

✱ *will, 'll* or nothing?

a ▶CD3 T38 **Listen and repeat.**

1 I'll go now.
2 She'll help you.
3 They'll be here on Monday.
4 You'll find out that I'm right.
5 The information will be on the Internet.
6 The universe will continue to get bigger.

b ▶CD3 T39 **Listen and write what you hear: *will*, *'ll* or – (nothing). Then listen again and check.**

1 Don't worry. I _'ll_ do this for you.
2 We _____ do our homework after lunch.
3 Ask Julia. She _____ know the answer.
4 The movie _____ start soon.
5 During a flight, the flight attendants _____ work very hard.
6 Go to college. I'm sure you _____ see how important it is for your future.
7 I doubt they _____ be here in half an hour.
8 They say that in the future, people _____ take vacations on the moon.

MOON VACATIONS
We'll fly you to the moon!

$1,200 for 3 nights!

4 Vocabulary

✱ Expressions to talk about the future

a **Make sentences from the words in the box for each situation below.**

| I think
I don't think | { | he'll give it back.
he'll know how to do it.
the baby will wake up.
they'll be late.
I'll finish before 9:00.
~~I'll enjoy it.~~ |

1 I want to watch this movie.
I think I'll enjoy it.
2 Please don't talk so loudly.
_____ .
3 Don't give your MP3 player to Travis.
_____ .
4 This exercise is hard! Let's talk to Sam.
_____ .
5 My friends will be here soon.
_____ .
6 It's 8:50, and I'm still doing my homework.
_____ .

b **Complete the sentences with the words in the box.**

doubt   hope   ~~probably~~   maybe   sure   not sure

1 Catherine _probably_ won't pass her test. She hasn't done much work.
2 I _____ Jaden will go to the concert. He doesn't enjoy pop music.
3 I sent the letter yesterday, but I'm _____ when it will arrive.
4 We don't know what we're doing in the summer, but _____ we'll go to Peru.
5 Tasha and John _____ to get married next year.
6 I bought a beautiful scarf for Amelia. I'm _____ she'll like it.

5 Culture in mind

Write the words in the correct column. Then check with the text on page 76 of the Student's Book.

cure diseases   no traffic jams   ~~cell phones~~   electric cars   Internet implants
virtual assistants   artificial parts   3-D conversations   online classes   plastic muscles

Communication	Health	Education	Transportation
cell phones	....	....	....
....	....	....	....
....	....		

6 Study help

✱ Using a dictionary (2)

a You can often use the same word as different parts of speech. For example, the word *joke* can be a noun or a verb. The dictionary shows this difference.

> **joke** /dʒəʊk/ *n* a funny story or trick to make people laugh: *Did I tell you the joke about the chicken crossing the road?*
> • a person or thing that is ridiculous or not nearly good enough: *Let's go home – this football game is a joke.*
> *v* to say funny things: *They joked and laughed as they looked at the photos.*

Which sentence uses *joke* as a verb? Which sentences use it as a noun? Write *v* or *n*.

1 No one can understand the instructions on this box. They're a **joke**! ......

2 Don't **joke** about this. It isn't funny. ......

3 I heard a very good **joke** on the radio yesterday. ......

b You can also see that a word often has more than one meaning. Sometimes the meanings are similar (for example, the two noun definitions for *joke*), but sometimes they are very different.

Read the dictionary entry for *land*. Then match the definitions with the sentences. Write a–d in the boxes.

> ⓐ **land** /lænd/ *n* the surface of <u>the earth</u> that is not covered by water: *It is cheaper to drill for oil on land than in*
> ⓑ *the ocean.* • <u>an area</u> in the countryside: *He has some land in the mountains. This land is good for growing fruit.*
> ⓒ *v* <u>to arrive</u> at a place after moving down through the air: *I always feel nervous*
> ⓓ *when the plane is landing.* • <u>to bring an aircraft down</u> to the earth's surface: *You can land a plane on water in an emergency.*

1 They grow wonderful tomatoes on their **land** in Tuscany. ☐

2 You can't **land** a helicopter in the middle of the forest! ☐

3 Hundreds of planes **land** at this airport every week. ☐

4 They couldn't see the **land** from the ship. ☐

7 Read

This is part of a story about a man named Adam. In 1712, he went to sleep in Boston, and when he woke up, it was 300 years later.

Read the story. Find the parts where Adam sees these things:

1   a CD store   *lines 18–21*
2   buses
3   a police officer
4   a police car
5   a TV store
6   cars
7   a clothing store
8   traffic lights

ADAM CAME OUT of the building and stopped. What was this awful place? The street was black. Strange boxes, made of metal and glass, moved quickly past him on wheels, making a terrible
5 noise. There were bigger boxes too, big yellow ones, with 10 or 20 children inside. Sometimes the boxes stopped. There were tall posts with three lights: red, yellow and green. The lights turned on and off, the boxes stopped and started again.
10 All around him, there were incredibly tall buildings. And the people! People everywhere. Many of them stopped and looked at him, then they turned and walked away quickly. Someone shouted to him, "Hey, you! Are you lost? The
15 theater's over there!" and then laughed. Adam walked past windows, big glass windows with women inside, but the women didn't move.

At the next window, he heard loud music coming through an open door. Inside he saw people looking at hundreds of little square boxes, 20 all with different pictures.

Then at another window, he saw larger boxes, this time with small people and houses *inside* them! Adam stopped again and looked around. One of the metal boxes on wheels was 25 near him – a black and white box with red and blue lights on top. A man in blue clothes and a hat got out and walked toward him. "Excuse me, sir," said the man. Adam didn't like him. He turned and ran.

WRITING TIP

Notice the way the text uses adjectives to create a clear picture and to show Adam's feelings. <u>Underline</u> all the <u>adjectives</u> in the first paragraph of the text. Then read the sentences without the adjectives and see how the picture loses life and color.

Use adjectives in your paragraph for Exercise 8. You can choose some from the box or use others that you know.

> dark   dangerous   strange   loud   huge
> frightening   angry   afraid   nervous

8 Write

After he ran away from the police officer, Adam went into a movie theater. Write the next paragraph of the story. Begin like this:

Adam ran through some big doors. A woman shouted, "Hey, you have to buy a ticket!" But Adam didn't stop. He pushed through a door and …

Unit check

1 Fill in the blanks

Complete the text with the words in the box.

| probably | won't | imagine | don't | she'll | to find | abroad | maybe | think | sure |

I know I _won't_ get good grades on my final exams, but I [1]_____ they'll be good enough for me to get into college. But before I start college, I'd like to go [2]_____ for a year. My friend Samantha and I will [3]_____ travel together in Asia and South America. When we come back, I think I'll study environmental science. I hope [4]_____ an interesting job after I graduate, but I [5]_____ think I'll be rich or famous! Samantha isn't [6]_____ what she'll do in the future. She's good at languages, so [7]_____ she'll become a translator or a language teacher, but who knows? I'm sure [8]_____ have lots of success in her life because she's a very intelligent person. [9]_____ us both being successful!

| | 9 |

2 Choose the correct answers

Circle the correct answer: a, b or c.

1 He isn't here yet, but I'm _____ he'll be here soon.

   a (sure)   b hope   c probably

2 When I'm older, I want to live _____ maybe in Japan.

   a away   b foreign   c abroad

3 I _____ I'll go out this weekend.

   a sure   b maybe   c doubt

4 My sister and her boyfriend are _____ married next month.

   a having   b doing   c getting

5 He has to work late, so he _____ won't come to the dance club.

   a maybe   b probably   c doubts

6 It's a beautiful morning. _____ it'll rain today.

   a I think   b I don't think   c I'm sure

7 They _____ to go to the University of Chicago next year.

   a hope   b think   c doubt

8 Steve got a bad grade on the test. His parents _____ be happy about that.

   a won't   b don't   c aren't

9 _____ find the information on the Internet?

   a We'll   b Do we will   c Will we

| | 8 |

How did you do?

Total: | | 25

3 Vocabulary

Circle the correct definition.

1 to imagine (verb)

   a to think about something that happened

   b to think about something that could happen

2 to read your mind (verb phrase)

   a to know what you're thinking

   b to turn something on

3 automatically

   a done by a machine

   b done by a person

4 virtual (adjective)

   a not real

   b friendly

5 to predict (verb)

   a to ask someone what will happen

   b to say what you think will happen

6 to cure (verb)

   a to make healthy

   b to hurt

7 implant (noun)

   a something put in the body

   b a type of phone

8 artificial (adjective)

   a outside the body

   b made by people

| | 8 |

| :) | Very good 25 – 20 | :| | OK 19 – 16 | :(| Review Unit 11 again 15 or less |

12 Don't give up.

1 Remember and check

The pictures show events from the text on page 78 of the Student's Book. Put them in the correct order. Write numbers 1–6 in the boxes. Then check with the text.

A `1`

B

C

D

E

F

2 Grammar

✱ *too* + adjective

a Match the sentences.

1 You won't get all your clothes in that bag.   a It's too long.
2 I won't finish this book tonight.   b I get too nervous.
3 I can't drive a car.   c It's too loud.
4 We can't swim here.   d It's too small.
5 I can't sleep before an exam.   e I'm too young.
6 Please turn the music down.   f The water is too polluted.

b Underline the correct words.

1 They're *very* / *too* old.

2 No, you can't play. You're *very* / *too* old.

3 Oh, no! It's *very* / *too* heavy.

4 Wow! This is *very* / *too* heavy!

5 I think she has a lot of money. Her car is *very* / *too* expensive.

6 It's *very* / *too* expensive for me. I only have $15.

c Alex is talking to Lucy, but he's saying some crazy things! Complete Lucy's replies. Use the verb *be* and an adjective from the box with *too*.

cold   easy   expensive   far   difficult   small   ~~old~~   young

1   **Alex:** It's my grandmother's 80th birthday tomorrow. I'm taking her to a dance club.

    Lucy: You can't do that! She *'s too old* .

2   **Alex:** I think I can learn to speak Chinese and Russian in six months.

    Lucy: No way! They _____ .

3   **Alex:** I'm going camping in Antarctica.

    Lucy: You're joking! It _____ .

4   **Alex:** I'm going for a ride on my little brother's bike.

    Lucy: You can't do that! It _____ for you.

5   **Alex:** My father wants to drive across Canada in two days.

    Lucy: That's impossible. It _____ .

6   **Alex:** Tomorrow I'm taking my six-year-old sister to a Dracula movie.

    Lucy: You can't do that. She _____ .

7   **Alex:** Look at this test! One of the questions is: *2 + 2 = ?*

    Lucy: I don't believe you! That _____ .

8   **Alex:** On Saturday, I'm buying some new shoes. They're $450.

    Lucy: $450? Oh, Alex, don't buy them. They _____ .

---

3 Vocabulary

✱ The weather

a Complete the text. Write the correct word in each space.

The weather on our vacation was a little strange. On the day we arrived, it was raining. It wasn't a lot, just a  _shower_ . But the next day, the ¹ _____ came out in the morning, and in the afternoon we stayed by the swimming pool because it was very ² _____ ! It was like that for another two days, but then, on the fifth day, there was a lot of ³ _____ in the evening. And at night, there was a terrible storm. We couldn't sleep because of the noise of the ⁴ **BOOM!** _____ , and we thought the ⁵ _____ was going to hit the hotel!

b **Vocabulary bank** Complete the words in the sentences.

1   It wasn't a lot of rain. It was just a l _i_ _g_ _h_ _t_ shower.

2   There was a very st _ _ _ _ wind, and a lot of trees fell down.

3   We couldn't see very much. The fog was really th _ _ _ on the roads.

4   It was a beautiful day yesterday with a lot of br _ _ _ _ sunshine!

5   You know it's going to rain when you see d _ _ _ clouds like those!

6   Sometimes, in January, we get very h _ _ _ _ snow in the mountains near here.

7   It isn't very windy today. There's just a g _ _ _ _ _ breeze.

8   I didn't sleep very well last night. There was a vi _ _ _ _ _ storm the whole night!

4 Grammar

✳ Adverbs

a Complete the table.

b Underline the correct words.

1 Work *quiet / quietly*, please.
  You're making too much noise.

2 I thought it was a *stupid / stupidly*
  movie, so I stopped watching it.

3 They walked *slow / slowly* across
  the park.

4 I won't go in Jack's car. He drives
  too *dangerous / dangerously*.

5 My *usual / usually* breakfast is
  coffee and toast.

6 To be *healthy / healthily*, you need
  to exercise.

Adjectives	Adverbs
quick	*quickly*
safe	1
2	noisily
3	early
hard	4
excellent	5
6	well
7	fast
easy	8
late	9

c Write sentences about the people in the pictures. Use a verb from box A and make
an adverb from the adjectives in box B.

A

| shout   work   play   win   ~~travel~~ |
| smile   get up   run |

B

| quick   happy   loud   hard   bad   late |
| easy   ~~slow~~ |

1 They*'re traveling slowly.*

2 She

3 He

4 The dogs

5 She

6 They

7 She

8 He

5 Pronunciation

✳ /ɔ/ and /oʊ/

a ▶**CD3 T40** Listen and repeat. Try to hear the difference between the /ɔ/ and the /oʊ/ sounds.

/ɔ/ job hot want foggy belong probably

/oʊ/ rope won't joke ki<u>lo</u> <u>go</u>ing nose

b ▶**CD3 T41** <u>Underline</u> the words or syllables with the /oʊ/ sound. (Circle) the words or syllables with the /ɔ/ sound. Then listen, check and repeat.

1 The (clock) is <u>older</u> than the (watch).
2 Bob and Tom don't go to the coast.
3 The foreign politician told a lot of jokes.
4 John wants to own a cell phone.
5 Those tomatoes are old.
6 Throw the potatoes in the pot!

6 Everyday English

Complete the dialogue with these expressions.

> in a way   ~~Not really~~   In fact   in a minute   the best thing to do   Are you sure

Mom: Hello, Ben! Are you OK?

Ben: Hi, Mom. Well, no. I'm not OK. _Not really._

M: What's wrong?

B: Well, I just don't feel very well. [1] ...., I feel awful.

M: Oh, no. Well, go to bed and relax, then. That's [2] ....

B: [3] .... ?

M: Absolutely! Go and lie down. I'll bring you a nice warm drink [4] ....

B: Thanks, Mom. You know, [5] ...., it's a good thing I don't feel well. We have an exam this morning at school.

M: Ben, are you really sick, or is this just a joke?

7 Study help

✳ Spelling and pronunciation

a It's often difficult to figure out the spelling of English words from their sound, or to be sure how to pronounce them from their spelling. But there are some patterns that you can follow. Here are some common spellings for the /oʊ/ sound.

o	ow	oa	o + consonant + e
g**o**	thr**ow**	c**oa**t	ph**o**ne
....	....	....	....
....	....	....	....
	....		....

b Add these words to the lists above:

> boat   tomorrow   potato   nose   joke   window   hello   soap   hope   follow

c You can make similar spelling lists for other sounds. For example, here are some common spellings for the /ər/ sound. Can you add more words to the lists?

er	ur	ir
v**er**b	t**ur**n	b**ir**d
....	....	....
....	....	....

- Look at your spelling lists regularly. Get used to the way the words look.
- Record difficult words. Then test yourself by listening and writing them down.

Skills in mind

8 Read

Read the questionnaire and choose the answers that are true for you.

How easily do you give up?

1 You have some very difficult homework to do. Do you …

a give up? ☐

b keep working at it? ☐

c go away and do something else, and then come back to the problem? ☐

2 You lend some money to a friend, but he/she doesn't give it back. Do you …

a stop talking to your friend? ☐

b forget about the money? ☐

c ask your friend (nicely) to give you the money as soon as possible? ☐

3 You see some clothes you really like, but they're very expensive. Do you …

a feel angry and try to forget the clothes? ☐

b buy something cheaper? ☐

c start saving money to buy the clothes that you really want? ☐

4 Your friend is angry with you, and you don't know why. Do you…

a forget about this friend and make new friends? ☐

b try to be nice to the friend even if he/she is angry? ☐

c ask the friend why he/she is angry and try to fix the problem? ☐

5 You want to play your favorite sport on the school team, but the coach never chooses you. Do you …

a decide not to play sports any more? ☐

b choose a different sport and try to get on that team? ☐

c practice harder and ask the coach why he/she doesn't choose you? ☐

Check your score

a = 0 points   b = 1 point   c = 2 points
8–10 points: Good for you! You don't give up easily.
4–7 points: Try a little harder to get the things you want.
0–3 points: Come on! You need to try, or you'll never get what you want!

9 Write

Choose one of the situations in the questionnaire and make it into a story. Write what happened.

WRITING TIP

Planning a narrative

- Plan the events in your story before you start to write. Use these questions to organize your ideas, and make notes for each question.

1 Setting the scene: where and when did the events happen?

2 What situation did you have to face?

3 What did you do first?

4 What happened after that?

5 How did it end?

- Follow the advice for brainstorming on page 24.

- When you are sure of the basic events, add some details to your plan. Try to "see" the situation as clearly as you can. What did things/people look like? How did people behave? How did you feel? Quickly write down words and phrases that you can use.

- Now use your notes to start writing your story. Write a paragraph for each question (1–5). Don't forget to:
  – use connectors *and*, *but* and *because* to link your ideas.
  – use adjectives and adverbs to give your story interest and color.

Unit check

1 Fill in the blanks

Complete the text with the words in the box.

> happily   snowed   windy   angry   weather   too   ~~rainy~~   sunny   really   heavily

Usually the winter is cold and __rainy__ in Chicago, so my family decided to take a weekend break in Miami last February. We wanted to enjoy some good weather. But when our plane landed in Miami, it was ¹_____ foggy to see anything through the windows. Before we got to our hotel, it started to rain ²_____ . On Saturday, the weather was worse. It was ³_____ and ⁴_____ cold. And on Sunday it ⁵_____ in Miami for the first time in 30 years! When we got back to Chicago that evening, my uncle met us at the airport. "The ⁶_____ was fantastic here this weekend," he said ⁷_____ . "It was warm and ⁸_____ every day! How was Miami?" My father was too ⁹_____ to answer him.

| 9 |

2 Choose the correct answers

(Circle) the correct answer: a, b or c.

1 It was really hot this afternoon, but it's nice and _____ now.

   a (cool)   b cold   c snowy

2 You have to drive slowly because there's a lot of _____ today.

   a sunny   b warm   c fog

3 Some trees fell over because of the _____ .

   a wind   b clouds   c sun

4 Don't forget your umbrella. They say it will _____ this afternoon.

   a rain   b rains   c raining

5 You can't learn to drive yet. You're _____ young.

   a too   b much   c very

6 They came _____ into the room.

   a quiet   b quietly   c too quiet

7 I can do this work _____ .

   a easy   b ease   c easily

8 We were in the airport for an hour because the plane arrived _____ .

   a late   b lately   c later

9 I'm really happy. My final grade was _____ .

   a very good   b too good   c very well

| 8 |

3 Vocabulary

Put the letters in the correct order to make words. Write the word(s) beside the sentence.

1 It was really *tho* yesterday afternoon. __hot__

2 Don't stay in the *uns* too long. You'll burn! _____

3 It wasn't heavy rain. It was light *rewosh*. _____

4 A: Did you see the *nihtginlg* last night? _____

5 B: No, but I heard the *derunth*! _____

6 *kiTch gof* makes it hard to drive safely. _____

7 What a beautiful day! I love *ritgbh uneshisn* like this! _____

8 The trees were all white this morning because there was *eyhva wons* last night.

   _____

9 I didn't sleep last night because there was a very *tenlovi mstor* all night! _____

| 8 |

How did you do?

Total: | | 25

| 🙂 | Very good
25 – 20 | 😐 | OK
19 – 16 | 🙁 | Review Unit 12 again
15 or less |

13 Promises, promises

1 Remember and check

Use the summary to fill in the puzzle. Check with the text on page 86 of the Student's Book.

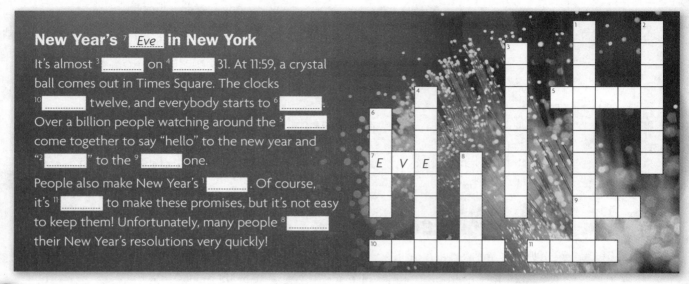

New Year's [7] _Eve_ **in New York**

It's almost [3] _____ on [4] _____ 31. At 11:59, a crystal ball comes out in Times Square. The clocks [10] _____ twelve, and everybody starts to [6] _____. Over a billion people watching around the [5] _____ come together to say "hello" to the new year and "[2] _____" to the [9] _____ one.

People also make New Year's [1] _____. Of course, it's [11] _____ to make these promises, but it's not easy to keep them! Unfortunately, many people [8] _____ their New Year's resolutions very quickly!

2 Vocabulary

✳ Multi-word verbs (2)

a Match the two parts of the sentences.

1 I want to take up skiing,   a but I couldn't find the answer.
2 My father gave up eating beef   b when you don't know what it means.
3 Look up a word in your dictionary c before I buy anything there.
4 The tennis match was called off   d so I'll have to buy some warm clothes.
5 I tried to work out the problem,   e because it was bad for his health.
6 I want to check out that new store f because it snowed all day.

> I need to do some exercise. I think I'll _____ _____ a new sport.

b Complete the sentences with the multi-word verbs. Use a word from each box.

work ~~look~~ call give take check   up out off

(1) Don't guess! _Look_ it _up_!

> Hey Andy. _____ _____ my new phone!

(2) Lesley, I think you'll have to _____ _____ skateboarding.

(3) Oh, no! It's 9:30! I might have to _____ _____ my plans with Todd.

(4) Can you _____ _____ where we are?

c Vocabulary bank Complete the sentences with *up*, *down*, *off*, *out* or *away*.

1 The fire alarm went ___off___ during the science exam.

2 Jessica! Remember to put your toys _____ after playing with them. I nearly fell over them and broke my leg!

3 The price of gas really went _____ last year. My mom complained every time she had to put gas in the car.

4 My cousins are coming to Atlanta next week and we're putting them _____ in our house! I can't wait!

5 It's raining, Oliver! We'll have to put your party _____ until next week. we can't celebrate in this weather!

3 Grammar

* be going to: intentions

a Steve is getting ready to go on vacation. Look at the picture and write *T* (true) or *F* (false).

1 Steve is going to take a vacation in Portugal. | F |
2 He's going to take his computer with him. | |
3 He isn't going to drive to Barcelona. | |
4 He's going to go snorkeling. | |
5 He's going to stay at a campsite. | |
6 He's going to take some photos. | |

b Complete the sentences with the correct form of *be* (affirmative or negative).

1 I _'m_ going to get up early tomorrow. I have to finish my French homework before school.

2 Greg _____ going to meet his sister at the bus station. She's arriving at 9:30.

3 _____ you going to watch the James Bond movie on TV tonight?

4 We don't have much money, so we _____ going to stay at an expensive hotel.

5 Jane _____ going to see the doctor because she's feeling much better now.

6 They have some sandwiches, cake and fruit juice. They _____ going to have lunch on the beach.

7 I _____ going to take the bus this afternoon. I want to walk home.

8 _____ your cousin going to come to the New Year's Eve party?

c Complete the questions with the correct form of *be going to* and the verbs in parentheses. Then complete the short answers.

1 A: ___Are___ your brothers _going to fly_ (fly) to Quito?

   B: No, ___they aren't.___

2 A: _____ Maria _____ (learn) to drive?

   B: Yes, _____ .

3 A: _____ Andrew _____ (move) to a new apartment?

   B: No, _____ .

4 A: _____ you _____ (wear) your red shirt tonight?

   B: No, _____ .

5 A: _____ Tim and Diane _____ (do) the dishes?

   B: Yes, _____ .

6 A: _____ we _____ (rent) a houseboat?

   B: Yes, _____ .

✱ *be going to*: predictions

d Complete the sentences. Use the correct form of *be going to* with the verbs in the box.

miss   have   ~~not snow~~   not enjoy   not see

1 It _isn't going to snow_ this afternoon.

2 I _____ this movie.

3 They _____ an argument.

4 We _____ anything up there.

5 We _____ the train!

e What's going to happen? Write sentences with *be going to* (affirmative or negative). Use your own ideas.

1 Come on! Your dinner is on the table.
   It's going to get cold.

2 Ella didn't get a good grade on her test.
   _____

3 No one can beat the Italian cyclists.
   _____

4 The car is out of control!
   _____

5 Stop climbing on that wall!
   _____

6 Patrick ate three hamburgers for lunch.
   _____

✱ *must/can't*

f Complete the school rules. Use *must* or *can't* and a verb in the box.

wear   use   be   do   bring   ~~eat~~

School rules

1 You _can't eat_ food during classes.
2 You _____ your homework.
3 You _____ your cell phone in the classroom.
4 Every student _____ a school uniform.
5 Students _____ pets to school.
6 Students _____ quiet when they are in the library.

BGS

BAYSIDE
GIRLS' SCHOOL

4 Pronunciation

✱ *be going to*

▶ **CD3 T42** Listen and check the words you hear. Then listen and repeat.

	go to	going to		go to	going to
1		✓	4		
2			5		
3			6		

5 Culture in mind

Complete the puzzle. Find the mystery name! Check with the text on page 90 of the Student's Book.

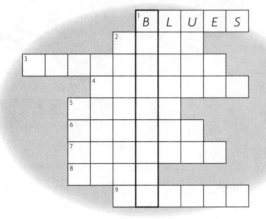

1 Reggae developed from rhythm and _blues_ music.

2 Reggae also developed from .... music.

3 People say that the beat of reggae is like the human ....

4 The island of .... is where reggae really became famous.

5 Many young people wanted to use reggae to fight for .... rights.

6 In the 1960s and 1970s, a lot of reggae songs got on the music ....

7 One of the most famous reggae bands was the ....

8 Reggae is often about "peace and ...."

9 For some people, the words or .... in reggae songs were very important.

6 Study help

✱ Speaking

Here are some ideas for speaking practice:

● Practice dialogues with a friend. If possible, record your dialogues, listen together and then practice again.

● Leave a voice message in English on your friend's phone. When you get a message from your friend, call back to leave a reply.

● If you know any English speakers, talk to them as often as you can.

● Try to talk in English for 5–10 minutes with a friend sometimes. You can write some questions to ask each other, for example:

Did you have a good day at school yesterday?

What was the weather like?

Who did you have lunch with?

Did you see [*someone's name*] yesterday?

Did you watch anything interesting on TV yesterday?

What did you do last weekend?

What are you going to do tomorrow?

With your friend, write down five more questions to ask each other.

....

....

....

....

....

Skills in mind

7 Listen

▶ CD3 T43 It's January 1st, and Denise is talking to her friend Robbie on the phone. Listen to the dialogue, and ⟨circle⟩ the correct letter: A, B or C.

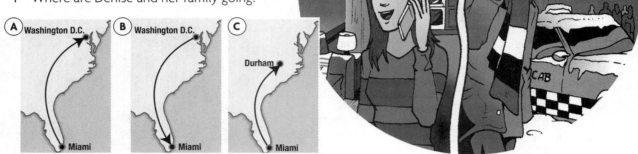

1 Where are Denise and her family going?

A Washington D.C. — Miami
B Washington D.C. — Miami
C Durham — Miami

2 When are they going to leave?

A next weekend B in about five weeks

C in about nine weeks

3 Which one is their new house?

 A FOR SALE 4 BEDROOMS & A POOL
 B FOR SALE 3 BEDROOMS & A POOL
 C FOR SALE 2 BEDROOMS & A POOL

4 How does Denise feel about selling the apartment?

 A
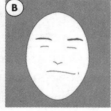 B
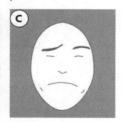 C

5 What is Denise's mother going to do?

 A
 B
 C

LISTENING TIP

Using audio scripts

For extra practice with this listening text, you can ask your teacher to give you the audio script.

- Use the audio script to listen and read at the same time. Pause after each person's speech, and read it aloud.

- Use white correction fluid to "white out" parts of the text. For example, you could remove all the verbs, or you could remove every sixth word. Perhaps your teacher will do this for you, or you could do it for a partner and then exchange audio scripts. A day or two later, listen to the recording again and try to fill in all the spaces.

8 Write

Imagine that you are Denise. Write an email to a different friend. Tell her about the things you and your family are going to do this year.

Unit check

1 Fill in the blanks

Complete the text with the words in the box.

| going | to | take | healthy | resolutions | call | ~~Year's~~ | give | isn't | must |

Now that it's New __Year's__ Day, everyone is making [1]_____ for the year. I want to get on the school basketball team this year, and that means I really [2]_____ get in shape. So I'm [3]_____ to start running in the morning before school. It [4]_____ going to be easy. I tried it once or twice last year, but I found it boring on my own, and I didn't keep it up. But this time, Brandon is going [5]_____ come running with me. I think this will help me to keep to my resolution, because if I [6]_____ it off, Brandon will be mad at me! He is determined to get in shape, too, so he says he's going to [7]_____ up hamburgers and chocolate. He's also going to [8]_____ up gymnastics. This is going to be the year of [9]_____ living!

☐ 9

2 Choose the correct answers

⊙ Circle the correct answer: a, b or c.

1 You must try to _____ up candy.
  a take b keep c (give)

2 They will call _____ the game if it rains.
  a off b out c up

3 It's a difficult question. Can you _____ the answer?
  a work out b take up c give up

4 It's getting late. _____ leave soon.
  a We must b Must we c We can't

5 Julio _____ going to meet us at the airport.
  a will b is c are

6 You _____ drive too fast in a school zone.
  a must b can't c going to

7 _____ Julia going to sing with the band?
  a Does b Will c Is

8 My brother is going to check _____ that new mall.
  a off b out c up

9 _____ they going to buy a new house?
  a Are b Is c Do

☐ 8

3 Vocabulary

<u>Underline</u> the correct words.

1 I don't know this word, so I'm going to look it *off / out / up*.

2 Hey, Diego. There's a great movie on TV! *Check / Look / Take* it out!

3 This song went on the music *lists / records / charts* last week.

4 Today's music is very different *as / than / from* music 30 years ago.

5 It's a great song. It's going to be a really big *hit / style / combination*.

6 This is my New Year's resolution: I'm going to give *off / up / out* chocolate.

7 The beat of this song is great, but I don't like the *lyrics / blues / records* very much.

8 It's a difficult problem, but I'm sure I can *look / take / work* out the answer.

9 Many people in the United States fought for *same / equal / every* rights for all people.

☐ 8

How did you do?

Total: ☐ 25

| 😊 | Very good 25 – 20 | 😐 | OK 19 – 16 | 🙁 | Review Unit 13 again 15 or less |

14 What a brave person!

1 Remember and check

Read the summary of Mr. Autrey's story. Complete it with the words in the box. Then check with the text on page 92 of the Student's Book.

> brave   dirty   ground   help   hospital
> ~~platform~~   right   serious   shocked
> young

One day Wesley Autrey was standing on the _platform_ of a subway station in New York City with his two [1] _____ daughters. He saw a man, Mr. Hollopeter, fall onto the track, and then he saw a train coming into the station.

Mr. Autrey jumped. He lay on top of the man and kept him down on the [2] _____ . The train traveled over them, but it didn't hit them. The people on the platform were [3] _____ .
Mr. Autrey shouted, "We're OK!" and then the other people started to clap and cheer.

Subway workers helped the two men out. An ambulance took Mr. Hollopeter to the [4] _____ . He had no [5] _____ injuries.

The only thing that happened to Mr. Autrey was that his blue hat got [6] _____ .

Later, Mr. Autrey said, "I wasn't [7] _____ . I didn't do anything special. I just saw someone who needed [8] _____ . I did what I thought was [9] _____ ."

2 Grammar

✻ First conditional

a Underline the correct words.

1 If _you finish_ / _you'll finish_ work before five, Olivia will take you home in her car.
2 They'll be disappointed if they _don't_ / _won't_ get concert tickets.
3 If Joshua wants to take a shower, _he has to_ / _he'll have to_ hurry.
4 If you don't wear a coat, _you're_ / _you'll be_ cold.
5 If Chris doesn't call Alexa tonight, _she sends_ / _she'll send_ him an email.

b Write first conditional sentences.

1 If / Hailey / miss / bus, / she / be / miserable

   If Hailey misses the bus, she'll be miserable.

2 If / train / not come soon, / we / walk home

   _____
   _____ .

3 You / not get wet / if you / wear / raincoat

   _____
   _____ .

4 I / not sing well / at concert / if I / be / too nervous

   _____
   _____ .

5 If / my friends / see me, / they / not recognize / me

   _____
   _____ .

c The pictures show people's possible plans for next Saturday. Complete the conditional sentences.

Christine

Michael

1 If the weather is nice, Christine
   _____
   _____ .

2 If it _____
   _____ .

3 If Michael _____
   _____ .

4 If he _____
   _____ .

d Think about your next free afternoon or evening, or your next weekend. Write three true sentences using the first conditional.

1 If ....

2 If ....

3 .... if ....

e Look at the pictures and complete the sentences. Use *will* or *won't* and the words in parentheses.

1 If he tries to climb up, ... (break)

2 If she goes into the yard, ... (attack her)

3 If we keep quiet, ... (find us)

4 If they drive too fast, ... (crash)

5 If you go to bed, ... (feel better)

6 If the weather gets worse, ... (take off)

✳ *when* and *if*

f Complete the sentences with *when* or *if*.

1 Nathan will look for a job __when__ summer vacation begins.

2 I'll do my homework .... I get home tonight.

3 We'll take a taxi .... Dad can't meet us at the station.

4 .... you waste time, you won't finish your work.

5 It'll be great .... I win this competition!

6 We'll have a big celebration .... it's your 21st birthday.

3 Pronunciation

✱ Stress in conditional sentences

a ▶CD3 T44 Listen to the sentences. <u>Underline</u> the stressed words or syllables.
Then listen again and repeat.

1 If he tries to get up, the train will hit him.
2 If he doesn't move, he'll be OK.
3 If I don't help him, the man will die.

b ▶CD3 T45 <u>Underline</u> the stressed words or syllables in the sentences in Exercise 2f.
Then listen, check and repeat.

4 Vocabulary

✱ Adjectives of feeling

a Match the two parts of the sentences.

1 My dog gets frightened   a so she's going to look for a new one.
2 Rosa's parents were annoyed   b about her birthday party next weekend.
3 She was tired   c when she hears fireworks.
4 I was interested   d after her long walk in the mountains.
5 She's bored with her job,   e because she got home late after the party.
6 My little sister is getting excited   f when I heard about the photography class.

b Complete the sentences with the adjectives in the box.

> annoyed exciting frightening worried ~~interesting~~ terrified

 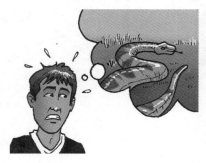 

1 This book isn't very
  interesting .

2 I'm ....
of snakes.

3 We can't find our cat. I'm
.... about him.

4 Our teacher gets
.... when
we don't listen.

5 It was a very
.... game.

6 There were strange
noises in the night. It was
....

C **Vocabulary bank** Put the letters in the correct order to complete the expressions about feelings and actions. Then fill in the crossword.

Across

4 When I'm frightened, I *racmse*. _scream_ .

7 When I'm worried, I rub my *rhafedoe*. _____

8 When I'm tired, I *wnay*. _____

Down

1 When you're excited, you *upjm* up and down.
   _____

2 When you're confused, you *tacschr* your head.
   _____

3 When you're angry, your face turns *edr*. _____

5 When you're bored, you *yradeadm*. _____

6 When you're nervous, you bite your *linsa*. _____

---

5 **Everyday English**

Circle the correct words.

1 A: I really want to ask Sarah out.

   B: So, ask her! Go *in* / *ahead*!

2 A: I got 85% on the French test.

   B: 85%? That's great. *Good job!* / *Job good!*

3 A: Oh, Dad. Can we please go to the soccer game this afternoon?

   B: No, Jimmy. The answer's "no," and *that's that* / *it's that*.

4 A: Look. It's not raining now.

   B: Great! So we can play tennis *after all* / *in the end*!

5 A: I can't give you back your money until next week. Sorry.

   B: That's OK. It's only ten dollars. It's not a *large thing* / *big deal*.

6 A: Wow! You said some really stupid things in class today!

   B: *Excuse you* / *Excuse me*? Don't talk to me like that, Chris!

---

6 **Study help**

✱ Grammar

Here are some things you can do to help you remember and review grammar.

● In your notebook, write down a grammar rule in the form of a diagram. For example:

First conditional

| If + present simple | + | will |

| will | + | if + simple present |

● Write example sentences that show the meaning clearly.

● Identify areas where you sometimes make mistakes. In your examples, highlight the difficult areas with different colored pens or highlighter pens.

● Go over the exercises in the Student's Book and Workbook.

● Record example sentences, and listen to them from time to time, for example, when you are doing the dishes or on your way to school.

● Work with a friend. Write some sentences on a particular grammar point, and include one grammar mistake in each sentence. Exchange your work, and correct the mistakes in your friend's sentences. Then discuss the sentences together.

Choose some or all of these points and use them to review the first conditional.

7 Read

a Read the school newspaper article, and put the pictures in the correct order. Write 1–5 in the boxes.

A

B

C

D
7

E

A medal for bravery

One of our students received a medal yesterday at the town hall for her bravery in helping an elderly lady.

Tonya Richards, 15, was in Lincoln in Brookport last May when she saw a pit-bull terrier that was barking furiously at an elderly woman, Mrs. Dana Stein. Mrs. Stein called for help, so Tonya ran closer and picked up some stones from the path.

"I started to throw stones at the dog," Tonya told us. "Then it turned around and started to come toward me. I was really scared. I stood still and shouted at the dog and it stopped, but it kept barking and looked very angry. I thought, "It's going to attack me!'"

At that moment, the dog's owner, Mr. Jeff Harris, arrived and called the dog off.

"Tonya is a very brave girl," commented Ms. Jackson, the mayor of Brookport, when she gave Tonya her medal. But Tonya says, "I don't really think I did anything special. The lady was clearly very frightened, so I just did the first thing I could think of."

Mr. Harris was fined $100 for not keeping his dog on a leash.

b Answer the questions.

1 Who did the dog bark at first?

   The dog barked at Mrs. Stein first.

2 What did Tonya throw at the dog?

   _____ .

3 What did the dog do next?

   _____ .

4 Why didn't the dog attack Tonya?

   _____ .

8 Write

Write a newspaper report about a person or people who did something brave. It can be about a true event, or you can invent one.

WRITING TIP

Organizing a newspaper report

Look at the text again. Notice that in the first paragraph of the report, the writer identifies the time and gives a very short general summary of the event. The report then gives a fuller description of the event with comments from Tonya and other people.

Follow the same pattern when you write your report. Think about the details before you begin to write. Make notes on these questions:

- Who was there?
- Where and when did it happen?
- What happened first?
- What happened next?
- Who said something about it?

Unit check

1 Fill in the blanks

Complete the message with the words in the box.

> I'm   I'll   tired   ~~interesting~~   interested   annoying   arrives   exciting   bored   when

How are you? Nothing _interesting_ is happening here, and I'm feeling [1]_____. There's nothing to do!
I started watching tennis on TV, but it wasn't very [2]_____, and I stopped watching. I can't go out
because I have to look after my little brother. It's [3]_____ because I had plans to go shopping with
Brooke this afternoon. Dad's at home, but he had to work all night at his job, so he's very [4]_____
now. Anyway, I can go out later [5]_____ Mom is home. If you're still [6]_____ in seeing the new
Spielberg movie, [7]_____ go with you. If Mom [8]_____ early, I'll meet you at the café at six.
But if [9]_____ not there, I'll see you at the theater before the movie starts. Is that OK?

| 9 |

2 Choose the correct answers

⊙ the correct answer: a, b or c.

1 I think it's a very _____ book.
   a interest **b** interested **c** (interesting)

2 Don't be _____ . You're safe here.
   a frighten **b** frightened **c** frightening

3 It's a dangerous situation, but we must try
   to stay _____ .
   a brave **b** tired **c** calm

4 Our car crashed and flipped over. It was _____ !
   a boring **b** terrifying **c** annoying

5 The bank _____ took $20,000.
   a robbers **b** fighters **c** jumpers

6 If the rope _____ , you'll fall.
   a breaks **b** will break **c** won't break

7 If they rent a car, _____ to Mexico.
   a they drive **b** they'll drive **c** they drove

8 The dog won't bite him if _____ move.
   a he'll **b** he won't **c** he doesn't

9 We'll feel more relaxed _____ final exams are
   over.
   a if **b** when **c** because

| 8 |

3 Vocabulary

Match the two parts of the words. Then
write the words in the correct places.

> pass   temp   ~~hosp~~   exci   exci
> ann   worr   terri   tir

> ted   ~~ital~~   oyed   fied   engers
> ed   erature   ting   ied

1 Three people were hurt in the crash and
   they went to the _hospital_ .

2 I think tomorrow's test is going to be
   difficult, so I'm a little _____ about
   it.

3 We're going on vacation tomorrow! I'm
   really _____ about it.

4 Can we stop for ten minutes, please? I'm
   really _____ and I need a break.

5 There was a problem with the plane, so
   all the _____ had to get off.

6 I can't pick that spider up! I'm
   _____ of spiders!

7 It's really hot in Egypt. Sometimes the
   _____ is 40°C!

8 That was a great movie. It was the most
   _____ one I've ever seen!

9 My brother dropped ice cream on my
   new pants. I was really _____ !

| 8 |

How did you do?

Total: | 25 |

| 😊 | Very good 25 – 20 | 😐 | OK 19 – 16 | 😟 | Review Unit 14 again 15 or less |

15 Travelers' tales

1 Grammar

✱ should/shouldn't

a Match the pictures with the sentences in the text. Write numbers 1–4 in the boxes. Then complete the sentences with *should* or *shouldn't*.

Take care of yourself!

1 You ___should___ go to bed early before a test.

2 You _____ eat plenty of fresh fruit and vegetables.

3 You _____ stand under a tree in a storm. There's a chance of lightning!

4 You _____ look left and right before crossing the street.

b Complete the sentences. Use the phrases in the box with *should* or *shouldn't*.

> take music lessons   eat a lot of candy
> talk to his teacher about it
> get a part-time job   go to bed late
> ~~be nice to people~~

1 Wendy doesn't have many friends. She
   should be nice to people.

2 Joe had three cavities in his teeth. He
   _____ .

3 Tim doesn't have much money. He
   _____ .

4 Adriana wants to be a singer. She
   _____ .

5 Julia is always tired when she gets up.
   She _____ .

6 Ryan doesn't understand his math
   homework. He _____
   _____ .

c Put the words in the correct order to complete the questions. Then write answers about the customs in your country.

1 you What say should
   What should you say when you meet someone
   for the first time?
   You should say _____ .

2 stand up students Should
   _____ when a teacher comes
   into the classroom?
   _____ .

3 present take Should you a
   _____ if someone invites you
   to her home?
   _____ .

4 you use should When
   _____ someone's first name?
   _____ .

5 shake Should hands people
   _____ when they meet
   someone for the first time?
   _____ .

6 person say a should What
   _____ if he/she steps on
   your foot?
   _____ .

d Give advice to these people. Write sentences starting with *You should* or *You shouldn't*.

1 I can't talk to my friend because she's in San Francisco.

You should write her a letter.

2 I feel sick today.

You ....

3 I want to speak English really well.

....

4 I have a science test tomorrow.

....

5 I want a really good job when I finish school.

....

6 Alex doesn't have any money.

....

2 Vocabulary

✱ Personality adjectives

a Look at the pictures. Complete the words to describe the people.

1 d _i_ _s_ _o_ _r_ _g_ _a_ _n_ _i_ _z_ _e_ _d_

2 h _ _ _ y

3 _ a _ _

4 _ _ l _ _ e

5 m _ _ _ _ _ _ b _ _

6 _ _ _ d-w _ _ _ _ _ _

7 _ _ g _ _ _ _ _ d

8 r _ _ _

9 n _ _ _ _ _ s

b ▶CD3 T46 Listen to Andy talking about some of the students in his class. <u>Underline</u> the adjective that describes each person.

Mario	**a** hard-working	**b** happy	**c** polite
Taylor	**a** honest	**b** kind	**c** friendly
Charlotte	**a** relaxed	**b** polite	**c** honest
Rachel	**a** helpful	**b** lazy	**c** mean
Max	**a** dishonest	**b** unfriendly	**c** lazy

c **Vocabulary bank** Write the words in the box next to the sentences.

> arrogant   bad-tempered   ~~easy-going~~   modest   outgoing
> shy   sympathetic   thoughtful   thoughtless   unsympathetic

1 She doesn't get upset about things. __easy-going__
2 He always thinks he's the best. _____
3 She always thinks about what other people want. _____
4 He makes new friends very easily. _____
5 She never talks about how good she is at things. _____
6 He doesn't care if you have had bad news. _____
7 She listens when you have bad news. _____
8 He often gets angry. _____
9 It's difficult for her to talk to other people. _____
10 He never thinks about what other people want. _____

3 Pronunciation
✱ Silent consonants

a ►CD3 T47 Listen to the word pairs. In one of the two words, the consonant in parentheses is silent. (Circle) the silent consonant. Then listen again, check and repeat.

1 (w) ans(w)er   twenty
2 (k) kind   knife
3 (t) often   faster
4 (n) autumn   station
5 (b) climber   robber
6 (h) hello   hour
7 (w) went   wrong
8 (l) hold   should
9 (c) science   vacation

b ►CD3 T48 (Circle) the silent letter. How should you pronounce the word? Listen, check and repeat.

1 lam(b)
2 could
3 castle
4 column
5 wrap

4 Grammar
✱ What's it like?

Read the answers and write questions with *What (be) ... like?* Use the words in the box.

> the weather   your new sunglasses   the party
> your neighbor   ~~the movie~~   Helen's friends

1 A: _What was the movie like?_
   B: It was great. It was really exciting, and the special effects were amazing.
2 A: _____ ?
   B: Well, they're sort of blue in color, and I think they're cool.
3 A: _____ ?
   B: It's cloudy and very cold. They say it's going to snow later.
4 A: _____ ?
   B: They were OK. They were pretty friendly, and some of them were interesting.
5 A: _____ ?
   B: I didn't enjoy it much. It was too crowded, and the music was awful.
6 A: _____ ?
   B: Oh, she's nice. She's really kind and friendly.

Vocabulary

✱ Adjectives for expressing opinions

a Match the adjectives that have similar meanings.

1	boring	a	horrible
2	great	b	nice
3	awful	c	dull
4	cool	d	fantastic

b Underline the correct adjectives.

1 A: What's that book like?

   B: It's OK, but it's a little _dull_ / horrible.

2 A: What's your new jacket like?

   B: It's *awful / cool*! I love it.

3 A: You should buy these.

   B: No, I think they're *attractive / ugly*.

4 A: Are you enjoying this show?

   B: No, it isn't very *boring / interesting*.

⑥ # Culture in mind

Complete the puzzle. Use the missing words in the text. Check with the text on page 104 of the Student's Book.

¹B	A	R	E	F	O	O	T
			²C				
		³	U				
⁴			A				
⁵			D				
		⁶	O				
⁷			R				

Ulises de la Cruz comes from Piquiucho, a small ⁴_____ in Ecuador, where most people live in simple ³_____ .

When he was young, he didn't have shoes or boots, so he played soccer ¹ _barefoot_ .

When Ulises got money for playing in the 2002 World Cup finals, he used it to buy a fresh ⁷_____ supply for Piquiucho. He has also set up a medical ²_____ there with doctors and nurses.

Ulises wants to help the ⁵_____ of Piquiucho, so that they can escape the ⁶_____ that they live in.

⑦ # Study help

✱ Vocabulary

It's a good idea to group adjectives with their opposites in your Vocabulary notebook.

a Find the opposites of the adjectives in the box, and write them in the lists. Use your dictionary if you need to.

> healthy   orderly   beautiful   obedient   usual
> quiet   lucky   stupid

dis-	*un-*	Different adjective
honest – dishonest	*kind – unkind*	*hard-working – lazy*

b Can you find the opposites to add to these lists? Use your dictionary to help you.

> useful   possible   perfect   careful

im-	*-less*
probable – improbable	*powerful – powerless*

Skills in mind

8 Read

Eu-nae is from Korea. After she finished school, she spent three months studying in the United States. Read her article giving advice to language students. Mark the statements *T* (true) or *F* (false).

I went abroad for the first time when I was 18. I traveled to the United States to study English, but I didn't learn to speak well. The main problem was that I made friends with other Korean people, so I spent too much time speaking Korean. It's important to make American friends and to spend a lot of time with your host family. If they have young children, it's even better. The children in my host family were great teachers.

Another problem was that I was worried about making mistakes when I spoke, so I didn't say much. But you shouldn't worry. American people are usually polite and helpful. You can't learn to say things if you don't talk. You should leave your dictionary at home and say what you can.

To help your listening, try to understand the conversations of people in stores and on buses.

I heard some very interesting things! Listening isn't easy at the beginning, but don't give up!

Read a magazine and watch a show on TV every day. All the students in my class did this, and it helped a lot. Of course, a movie is a fun way to practice your English. Listening to songs is helpful, too. There are lots of good American bands.

Finally, don't study too hard. Give yourself a lot of time for fun, but try to have fun in English!

1 Eu-nae didn't go to other countries when she was a young child. `T`

2 She spoke English well after studying in the U.S. `F`

3 She had a lot of American friends. ☐

4 The children in her host family didn't help her. ☐

5 She thinks students should always carry a dictionary with them. ☐

6 She listened to people talking when she went shopping. ☐

7 She thinks it's a good idea to watch TV every day. ☐

8 She believes students should always study very hard. ☐

9 Write

Use Eu-nae's advice to make a poster.

Going abroad to study English? Remember this advice!
You should …
spend a lot of time with your host family.
You shouldn't …
make friends only with people from your country.

READING TIP

Answering true/false *questions*

- Read the statements very carefully. It's important to know exactly what they are saying before you decide if they are true or false. <u>Underline</u> key words and phrases. Also look out for negatives. If you miss these, you will get the wrong answers.

- Read the examples. Why are they true or false? Look through the text to find the parts that give the answers ("I went abroad for the first time when I was 18," "I didn't learn to speak well"). Look out for expressions that are similar in meaning (for example, "go to other countries" – "went abroad"). Do the same with the rest of the statements.

Unit check

1 Fill in the blanks

Complete the dialogue with the words in the box.

> dishonest   should   miserable   kind   ~~nervous~~   disorganized   shouldn't   lazy   happy   like

A: The final exams are in two days, but Gino isn't _nervous_ at all.

B: I know. He's amazing! He's always relaxed and [1] _____ , so he never stops smiling. Even when bad things happen, he isn't [2] _____ .

A: Julie thinks he's [3] _____ . She says he never does any work.

B: That isn't true. You [4] _____ listen to Julie. She's often [5] _____ , so you can't believe half the things she says.

A: You know Gino's brother, don't you? What's he [6] _____ ?

B: Well, he's incredibly [7] _____ . He's always late, and he's always losing things. But he's very [8] _____ . He thinks about people and does a lot to help them. You [9] _____ meet him. He's a nice guy.

| 9 |

2 Choose the correct answers

(Circle) the correct answer: a, b or c.

1 He was _____ . He really hurt my feelings.

  a (mean)   b nervous   c friendly

2 I'm sure her story is true. She's a very _____ person.

  a rude   b hard-working   c honest

3 Our neighbors never speak to us. They're very

  _____ .

  a miserable   b kind   c unfriendly

4 You're going to love this music. It's _____ .

  a horrible   b great   c attractive

5 The party was _____ and boring.

  a dull   b cool   c ugly

6 You _____ wear those jeans. They're too short.

  a must   b should   c shouldn't

7 That bike isn't very safe. I don't think he _____ ride it.

  a should   b must   c shouldn't

8 _____ buy this book for Dad's birthday?

  a We should   b Should we   c Do we should

9 A: _____ the weather like?   B: It's awful!

  a What was   b What's   c What does

| 8 |

3 Vocabulary

Write the opposites of the words.

1 kind   _____mean_____

2 organized   _____

3 honest   _____

4 polite   _____

5 lazy   _____

6 nervous   _____

7 attractive   _____

8 outgoing   _____

9 thoughtful   _____

| 8 |

How did you do?

Total: | 25 |

| :) Very good 25 – 20 | :\| OK 19 – 16 | :(Review Unit 15 again 15 or less |

1 Remember and check

a Match the three parts of the sentences. Check with the text on page 106 of the Student's Book.

1	Lee Redmond's fingernails	uses	snow angels at the same time.
2	In 2004, 15,851 people	grew	110 meters.
3	The Miniature Wunderland train	measures	1.5 million toothpicks.
4	Saimir Strati's picture	made	to be 8.65 m long.

b Look at the pictures. Complete the sentences. Use the verbs from the middle column in Exercise 1a.

1 We __*made*__ our own costumes for the party.

2 My younger brother _____ a lot in the last six months!

3 My dad grew a carrot that _____ 1.5 meters!

4 Our dog _____ over 40 kilos!

2 Grammar

✻ Present perfect

a Complete the sentences. Use the past participle form of the verbs in the box.

> ~~play~~ eat drive listen work write do learn

1 Michael has often __*played*__ basketball at the gym.

2 My mother has _____ at a lot of different jobs.

3 I've never _____ a car.

4 Liz has _____ how to fly a plane.

5 We've _____ Spanish food once or twice.

6 My cousin has never _____ an email to me.

7 You've _____ to the new song.

8 My brothers have always _____ the housework at home.

Underline the correct words.

1 I've *read* / *reading* this book three times.

2 This actress has *been* / *being* in about 30 movies.

3 Annette and Luke *has* / *have* never played hockey.

4 Martin hasn't *spoke* / *spoken* to the teacher.

5 We *never been* / *have never been* in a helicopter.

6 *Have you traveled* / *Have you travel* to a lot of countries?

c **Put the words in the correct order to make questions and answers.**

1 A: your Has father competition won ever a

   Has your father ever won a competition?

   B: won he's anything No, never

   No, he's never won anything.

2 A: ever snake you Has a bitten

   .... ?

   B: snake I've a No, never seen even

   ....

3 A: flown to you Have the United States ever

   .... ?

   B: never in I've plane No, been a

   ....

4 A: in your swum this friends pool Have

   .... ?

   B: they've swim never to learned No,

   ....

d **Use the words to write questions. Then write the short answer that is true for you.**

1 see / a tiger?

   A: *Have you ever seen a tiger?*

   B: *Yes I have / No I haven't.*

2 meet / a pop star?

   A: ....

   B: ....

3 eat / Mexican food?

   A: ....

   B: ....

4 try / windsurfing?

   A: ....

   B: ....

5 be / in the hospital?

   A: ....

   B: ....

e **Complete the dialogue. Use the present perfect form of the verbs in parentheses.**

Lauren: Jesse! I *'ve never seen* (never see) you looking so happy. Is this your new bike?

Jesse: Yeah. Isn't it great? I [1] .... (never have) such a good bike before.

Lauren: Does it work OK? [2] .... you .... (have) any problems with it?

Jesse: No, it works really well. Hey, why don't we go for a long ride, out to Moorsby Park?

Lauren: Moorsby Park? I [3] .... (never be) there.

Jesse: Oh, it's really nice. Dad and I [4] .... (drive) there a few times in the car. It's about 20 kilometers from here.

Lauren: Wow! I [5] .... (never cycle) that far.

Jesse: Don't worry, a little bike ride [6] .... (never kill) anyone! We'll be back by lunchtime. Then we can go and get some food at the Mexican fast-food place. We can have nachos. [7] .... you .... (ever eat) nachos?

Lauren: Yeah, lots of times. I love them. OK, let's go!

3 Pronunciation

✱ *have* and *has* in the present perfect

▶CD3 T49 Listen and check (✓) the sentence you hear. Then listen again and repeat.

1 I cut my finger. ☐
   I've cut my finger. ☐

2 Did you see the parrot? ☐
   Have you seen the parrot? ☐

3 He told the teacher. ✓
   He's told the teacher. ☐

4 They won a lot of prizes. ☐
   They've won a lot of prizes. ☐

5 He's seeing the doctor. ☐
   He's seen the doctor. ☐

6 She's eating the chocolate. ☐
   She's eaten the chocolate. ☐

4 Vocabulary

✱ Verb and noun pairs

a Complete the sentences. Use a word from each box.

raise	~~win~~	break	told	took	build

the record	a house	a risk	a joke	~~a prize~~	money

1 We should enter the competition. Maybe we'll _win a prize_ .

2 You _____ when you went skating on the river. The ice was really thin.

3 It's a charity concert. They want to _____ for the Red Cross.

4 She's training hard, and her times are excellent. She's sure she'll win the 800-meter race, and she also hopes to _____ .

5 I _____ , but nobody laughed.

6 My parents bought a piece of land, and they want to _____ on it next year.

b **Vocabulary bank** Write the nouns in the correct verb column.

(someone) a hand   an argument   a mess   the time   ~~(the) housework~~   an effort
a presentation   the truth   a break   an exam   an accident   your best

do	give	have	make	take	tell
(the) housework					

c Complete the sentences with a verb in its correct form from the table in Exercise 4b.

1 I dropped a plate of food on the kitchen floor, and it _made_ a real mess.

2 I didn't win the race, but that's OK. I know that I _____ my best.

3 It's been a tiring day so far. Let's _____ a break for half an hour.

4 Caleb and I aren't talking to each other. We _____ a really big argument last week.

5 If you do something wrong, the best thing to do is to _____ the truth about it.

6 I really enjoy _____ presentations in class.

✻ Expressions about *sleep*

d Use the words in the three columns to make five more sentences.

1 *I went to sleep as soon as I got into bed.*
2 _____
3 _____
4 _____
5 _____
6 _____

I went	a dream	so please be quiet. I don't want her to wake up.
Joe went	asleep	about flying.
The baby is	to sleep	as soon as I got into bed.
Maria had	to bed	so you don't have to be quiet.
	awake	at work, and his boss wasn't very happy.
		at midnight, but I read until two in the morning.

5 Everyday English

1 A: Do you want to go to the café?

   B: *Definitely* !

2 Let's go to the mall. We haven't gone in a _____ .

3 A: What's for dinner, Mom?

   B: _____ and see! It's something special.

4 This movie is boring. Tell you _____ . Let's go for a walk.

5→ Hey, _____ what you say. You might hurt Jen's feelings.

5↓ We want to go to a restaurant tonight. By the _____ , do you know any good Italian places?

```
        D
 2 □□□□ E
        F
 3 □□□  I
        N
        I    4
 5 □□□ T □
        E
        L
        Y
```

6 Study help

✻ Grammar

For irregular verbs, learn the past participle with the simple past form.
It's a good idea to divide the verbs into groups:

No change

Base form	Simple past	Past participle
put	put	put
___	___	___

Different past participle

Base form	Simple past	Past participle
speak	spoke	spoken
___	___	___
___	___	___
___	___	___

Same simple past and past participle

Base form	Simple past	Past participle
have	had	had
___	___	___
___	___	___

Write the three forms of these verbs in the correct lists.

write   fly   make   cut   meet   drive   go

Keep lists like this in your notebook, and add to them. Go through your lists regularly, and say the three verb forms aloud. You can also record them and listen to them regularly.

7 Read and listen

▶CD3 T50 Here are two jokes. Read and listen, and complete the texts.

A man goes into a pizza place and asks for a pizza. The girl asks him what he wants on it.

"Oh, ham and ¹ _____ and olives, please."

"Fine," says the girl. "And what size pizza

² _____ _____ _____ ?"

"What sizes do you have?" asks the man.

"Well, you can have small, medium or large."

"Oh," says the man. "Um ... medium, ³ _____ ."

The girl says, "OK. And do you want me to

⁴ _____ it into ⁵ _____ pieces or

⁶ _____ pieces?"

The man thinks about it and says, "Just four pieces, please. I'm not really very hungry. I don't think I

⁷ _____ _____ _____

_____ !"

8 Write

Write a funny story. It can be:

- something that really happened to you or someone you know

- a joke that you know

- something that happened in a movie or a book

- a story that you make up yourself

Try to plan your story so that the funniest part comes at the end.

Two farmers go out one day, and they buy two horses, one each. They put the two horses in a field.

"Wait a minute," says one farmer. "How will we know which horse is yours and which horse is

⁸ _____ ?"

So the two farmers sit down and think about it. They ⁹ _____ to paint the horses' tails. One tail will be ¹⁰ _____ , and the other tail will be ¹¹ _____ .

But that night, it ¹² _____ and the paint comes off. So the two farmers think about it again. Then one of them says, "Oh, what stupid farmers we are! Look, it's easy. Your ¹³ _____ _____ is

¹⁴ _____ _____

my ¹⁵ _____ _____ !"

WRITING TIP

Checking and self-correction

When you finish writing, look it over to check for errors. Ask yourself these questions:

- Have I put the events in a logical order?

- Does my story include all the necessary information? Do I need to add anything?

- Where do I often make grammar mistakes? Have I made any mistakes this time?

- Is my spelling correct? Do I need to check the dictionary?

- Have I used the correct words to say what I mean? Could I use better words in some places?

- Will my reader understand and enjoy my story?

Unit check

1 Fill in the blanks

Complete the text with the words in the box.

> ever   never   haven't   ~~has~~   truth   was   been   snake   risk   spoken

My brother Danny ___*has*___ always loved animals, and when he was younger, he had a lot of different pets.
The most dangerous was a ¹ _____ named Sting. I've ² _____ liked snakes, and I thought Danny
was taking a ³ _____ when he got it. So, when I say that I was happy when Sting finally died two years
ago, I'm telling the ⁴ _____ ! Now Danny's only pets are two green parrots called Posh and Becks.
Usually these birds imitate human voices, but, strangely, Posh and Becks have ⁵ _____ only once in
their lives. A month ago, I ⁶ _____ in Danny's room and asked him, "Have you ⁷ _____ thought
about selling those parrots?" Before he could answer, Posh said loudly, "No way!" and Becks said,
"You must be crazy!" I've never ⁸ _____ so amazed! Since then, those parrots ⁹ _____ said
another word.

`9`

2 Choose the correct answers

(Circle) the correct answer: a, b or c.

1 He _____ first prize in the competition.
   a (won)   b raised   c had

2 They _____ a lot of money for charity.
   a took   b won   c raised

3 Irena always _____ horrible jokes!
   a says   b tells   c speaks

4 He ran very fast, but he didn't _____ the record.
   a build   b break   c win

5 _____ your sister three or four times.
   a I meet   b I've met   c I've never met

6 My grandparents _____ flown in a plane.
   a have never   b has never   c haven't never

7 Jenny hasn't _____ Indian curry.
   a eat   b ate   c eaten

8 Have you ever _____ a tiger?
   a see   b seen   c saw

9 You're _____ a big risk if you ride your bike
   at night.
   a doing   b making   c taking

`8`

3 Vocabulary

Fill in the crossword.

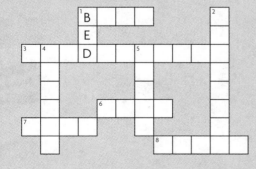

1 ↓ What time did you go to ___*bed*___ last night?

1 → Don't worry about the exam tomorrow. Just do your _____ , OK?

2 I got angry with her, and we had a big _____ .

3 Sometimes I sit and look out of the window, just _____ .

4 Please don't make any noise. The baby's _____ .

5 I went to bed at 10:30, but I was _____ until midnight.

6 Please be careful! Don't _____ any risks!

7 We made a _____ in the living room, so we had to clean it up.

8 Tell me the _____ . Did you break my camera?

`8`

How did you do?

Total: `25`

Very good 25 – 20	OK 19 – 16	Review Unit 16 again 15 or less	

Vocabulary bank

Unit 3 hobbies and interests

1 keeping a journal

6 collecting stickers (stamps/coins)

2 bird-watching

7 drawing pictures

3 hanging out with friends

8 making models

4 going for walks

9 fishing

5 taking care of a cat (dog/rabbit)

10 doing puzzles

Unit 4 housework

1 a pillow	4 a (cleaning) cloth	7 (book) shelves	10 (dresser) drawers	13 (clothes) hangers
2 a comforter	5 a mop	8 a magazine rack	11 a cupboard	14 a trash can
3 a vacuum cleaner	6 a bucket	9 a CD rack	12 a wardrobe	15 a poster

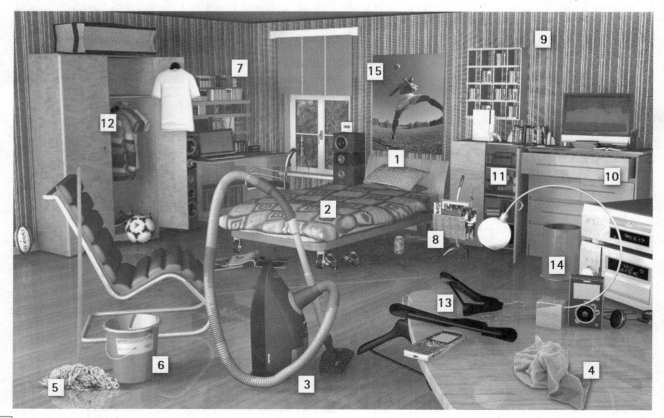

Unit 5 multi-word verbs (1) (with up, down, on, off)

1 to get up

2 to stand up

3 to sit down

4 to lie down

5 to get on

6 to get off

7 to turn on

8 to turn off

Unit 6 sports equipment and places

1 a helmet

2 boxing (cycling/ goalie/golf) gloves

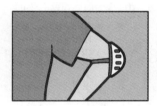
3 (knee/elbow/ shin) pads

4 a tennis (squash/ badminton) racket

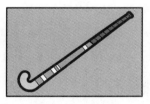
5 a field hockey (lacrosse/polo) stick

6 a soccer (baseball) shoe

7 soccer (tennis/rugby) shorts

8 a soccer (tennis/rugby) shirt

9 a surf (skate) board

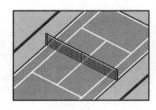
10 a tennis (squash/ volleyball) court

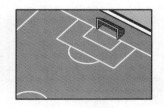
11 a soccer (rugby/ baseball) field

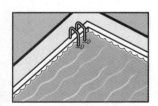
12 a swimming pool

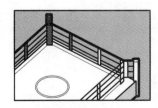
13 a (boxing) ring

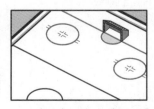
14 a hockey (ice skating) rink

15 a gym

Unit 7 work

1 (to work) at home

2 (to work) in an office

3 (to work) in a store

4 (to work) in a factory

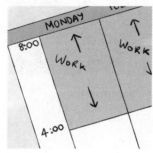

5 (to work) a day shift

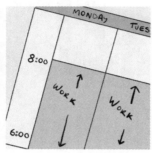

6 (to work) a night shift

7 (to earn) an hourly wage

8 (to earn) a salary

Unit 8 food / things we use to eat and drink

1 a knife

2 a fork

3 a spoon

4 a plate

5 a glass

6 a bowl

7 a napkin

8 a cup

9 a saucer

10 a dish

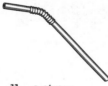

11 a straw

12 chopsticks

13 a mug

14 a menu

Unit 10 vacation activities

1 taking photographs
2 going to a market
3 looking at a view
4 visiting monuments
5 trying local food
6 meeting local people
7 buying souvenirs
8 trying to speak the language
9 going on an excursion
10 learning local customs
11 visiting a theme park
12 learning about history and culture

Unit 12 adjectives to talk about the weather

1 bright sunshine   2 dark clouds   3 heavy rain   4 a light shower   5 a strong wind

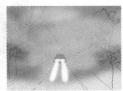

6 a gentle breeze   7 thick fog   8 a thin mist   9 heavy snow   10 a violent storm

Unit 13 multi-word verbs (2) (with *go* and *put*)

1. put (a fire) out = stop a fire burning

   It was a very bad fire. The firefighters finally **put** it **out** after six hours.

2. put (someone) up = give them a place to stay or sleep

   We're coming to Los Angeles next week. Can you **put** us **up** in your house for a few days?

3. put (something) off = change something to a later date

   It was raining very badly, so we **put** the soccer game **off** until next week.

4. put away = clean

   This room's a mess. Can you **put** everything **away**, please?

5. go up = increase

   The price of food **has gone up** a lot recently.

6. go down = decrease

   My math grade **went down** this year. Last year I got a B, this year I got a C.

7. go off = explode

   The firecrackers **went off** at midnight.

8. go off = ring

   My alarm clock **didn't go off** this morning.

Unit 14 feelings and actions

1. When I'm bored (or tired), I start to **yawn**.

2. When she's bored, she starts to **daydream**.

3. When the kids are excited, they **jump up and down** and **clap their hands**.

4. When I'm frightened, I **close my eyes**.

5. Some people **scream** when they're frightened.

6. He's very confused. Look, he's **scratching his head**.

7. She's very nervous. She's **biting her nails**.

8. When I get nervous, I start to **pace** the room.

9. I think he's angry. His **face turned red**.

10. When he's worried, he often **rubs his forehead**.

Unit 15 personality adjectives

1 He doesn't get angry or upset about things. He's very **easy-going**.

2 She gets angry all the time. She's very **bad-tempered**.

3 She always thinks about what other people want. She's really **thoughtful**.

4 He never thinks about what other people want. He's really **thoughtless**.

5 She listens when you have problems or bad news. She's very **sympathetic**.

6 He doesn't care if you have bad news. He's very **unsympathetic**.

7 He never talks about how good he is at things. He's very **modest**.

8 She always talks about how she's the best. She's really **arrogant**.

9 It isn't very easy for him to talk to other people. He's pretty **shy**.

10 She makes new friends very easily. She's very **outgoing**.

Unit 16 verb and noun pairs

1 to make a mess

2 to make an effort

3 to do (the) housework

4 to do your best

5 to have an argument

6 to have an accident

7 to take a break

8 to take an exam

9 to give a talk/presentation/ speech

10 to give (someone) a hand

11 to tell the time

12 to tell the truth

It's true – honestly!

Grammar reference

Unit 3

Simple present (affirmative and negative; questions and short answers)

1   We use the simple present for actions that happen repeatedly or habitually.

*Sally often **goes** to the swimming pool.*   *We **have** breakfast at 7:30 every morning.*

We also use the simple present for things that are always or normally true.

*Apples **grow** on trees.*   *He **lives** in Italy.*

2   With most subjects, the simple present is the same as the base form of the verb. However, with a third person singular subject (*he, she, it*), the verb has an *s* ending.

*I **play** tennis on Fridays.*   *She **plays** tennis on Fridays.*
*My parents **work** in Boston.*   *My brother **works** in Boston.*

If a verb ends with *sh, ch, ss* or *x*, we add *es*.

*he wash**es**   she catch**es**   he miss**es**   she fix**es***

If a verb ends with consonant + *y*, we change the *y* to *i* and add *es*.

*she stud**ies**   he worr**ies***

3   The negative of the simple present is formed with *don't* (*do not*) or *doesn't* (*does not*) + base form of the verb.

*I **don't like** fish.*   *She **doesn't like** fish.*
*Students **don't wear** uniforms.*   *Jack **doesn't wear** a uniform.*

4   Simple present questions and short answers are formed with *do* or *does*.

***Do** you **like** cats?*   *Yes, I **do**. / No, I **don't**.*
***Do** they **play** the guitar?*   *Yes, they **do**. / No, they **don't**.*
***Does** Silvia **live** here?*   *Yes, she **does**. / No, she **doesn't**.*

like + -ing

1   After verbs that show liking and not liking we often use verb + *-ing*.

*We **love going** to the movies.*   *My parents **hate going** to the supermarket.*
*My sister **enjoys watching** DVDs at home.*   *I **don't like doing** my homework.*

2   If a verb ends in *e*, we drop the *e* before adding *-ing*.

live – living   ride – riding

If a short verb ends in 1 vowel + 1 consonant, we double the final consonant before adding *-ing*.

*get – ge**tt**ing   shop – sho**pp**ing*

Unit 4

Present continuous for activities happening now

1   We use the present continuous for actions that are happening now or around the time of speaking.

*My brothers **are watching** TV right now.*
*It'**s raining** now.*

2   The present continuous is formed with the simple present of *be* + verb + *ing*.

*I'**m enjoying** this book.*   *I'**m not enjoying** this book.*
*You'**re working** very hard!*   *You **aren't working** very hard.*
*Alison **is listening** to music.*   *Alison **isn't listening** to music.*

3   The question is formed with the simple present of *be* + subject + verb + *ing*.

***Is** Carlo **reading**?*   *Yes, he **is**. / No, he **isn't**.*
***Are** the girls **having** lunch?*   *Yes, they **are**. / No, they **aren't**.*
*What **are** you **doing**?*
*Why **is** she **laughing**?*

Simple present vs. present continuous

1   Time expressions for repeated actions are often used with the simple present.

Time expressions for present or temporary actions are often used with the present continuous.

Simple present	Present continuous
every day *on Mondays* *on the weekend*	*today* *tonight* *this afternoon* *this weekend*
usually *sometimes* *often* *never*	*right now* *at the moment* *today*

2   Some verbs aren't normally used in the continuous form. Here are some common examples:

believe   know   understand   remember   want   need   mean   like   hate
*I **remember** you.*   *We **need** some milk.*   *David **loves** pasta.*

Unit 5

Simple past: *be*

1   We use the simple past to talk about actions and events in the past.

2   The simple past of *be* is *was/wasn't* or *were/weren't*.

*I **was** in town yesterday.*   *My sister **wasn't** with me.*
*We **were** at a friend's house last night.*   *We watched some movies, but they **weren't** very good.*

3   Questions with *was/were* are formed by putting the verb before the subject.

***Were** you in the park yesterday?*   ***Was** Jason with you?*

Simple past: regular verbs

1   In the simple past, regular verbs have an *ed* ending. The form is the same for all subjects.

*I walk**ed** to the park.*   *You play**ed** soccer well yesterday.*
*Carla open**ed** the window.*   *It start**ed** to rain in the afternoon.*

If a verb ends in *e*, we add only *d*: *like – liked   hate – hated   use – used*

If a verb ends with consonant + *y*, we change the *y* to *i* and add *ed*.

*study – stud**ied**   try – tr**ied**   marry – marr**ied***

If a short verb ends in 1 vowel + 1 consonant, we double the final consonant before adding *ed*.

*stop – stop**ped**   plan – plan**ned***

2   The negative of the simple past is *didn't* (*did not*) + base form of the verb. This is the same for all subjects.

*I **didn't like** the movie last night.*   *He **didn't study** last night.*
*We **didn't walk** to school.*   *The bus **didn't stop** for me.*

3   Past time expressions are often used with the simple past.

yesterday   yesterday morning   last night   last week   a month ago   two years ago   on Sunday

Unit 6

Simple past: regular and irregular verbs

A lot of common verbs are irregular. This means that the simple past form is different. Irregular verbs don't have the usual *ed* ending. There is a list of irregular verbs on page 122 of the Student's Book.

*go – **went**   see – **saw**   eat – **ate**   think – **thought***

Simple past: questions and short answers

Simple past questions and short answers are formed with *did*. The form is the same for regular and irregular verbs.

***Did** you **talk** to Barbara this morning?*   *Yes, I **did**. / No, I **didn't**.*
***Did** they **play** tennis yesterday?*   *Yes, they **did**. / No, they **didn't**.*
***Did** Bruno **go** home after the party?*   *Yes, he **did**. / No, he **didn't**.*

Unit 7

have to / don't have to

1   We use *have to* to say that it is necessary or very important to do something.
    *I'm late. I **have to** go now.   We **have to** be at school at 8:30.*

    With a third person singular subject (*he, she, it*), we use *has* to.
    *Jimmy is very sick. He **has to** stay in bed.   My mother **has to** go to Toronto tomorrow for a meeting.*

2   We use the negative form *don't/doesn't have to* to say that it isn't necessary or important to do something.
    *It's early, so I **don't have to** hurry.   Diana **doesn't have to** get up early on Sundays.*

3   Questions are formed with *do* or *does*: ***Do** I **have to** go to school?   **Does** he **have to** pay?*

4   The past form is *had to / didn't have to*. The form is the same for all subjects.
    *Joanna **had to** go to the dentist last week.*
    *Yesterday was a holiday, so we **didn't have to** go to school.*
    ***Did** you **have to** iron the clothes last night?*

5   All forms of *have to* are followed by the base form of the verb.

Unit 8

Count and noncount nouns

1   Nouns in English are count or noncount. Count nouns have a singular and a plural form.
    car – cars   house – houses   apple – apples   question – questions
    man – men   woman – women   child – children   person – people

2   Noncount nouns don't have a plural form. They are singular.
    food   music   money   rice   bread   information
    *This **food is** horrible.   This **information is** wrong.*

3   Sometimes a noun can be count or noncount, depending on its meaning in the sentence.
    *I like **coffee**. (noncount)   I'd like two **coffees**, please. (= two cups of coffee, count)*

a/an and some

1   With singular count nouns, we can use *a/an* to indicate a nonspecific thing or person.
    *They live in **an apartment**.   He's carrying **an umbrella**.*

    With plural count nouns, we use *some*: *I want to buy **some eggs**.*

2   With noncount nouns, we don't use *a/an*. We use *some*: *Let's have **some bread**.*

much and many

1   We use *many* with plural count nouns and *much* with noncount nouns.

Count	Noncount
*She doesn't eat **many vegetables**.*	*He doesn't eat **much fruit**.*
*How **many children** do they have?*	*How **much time** do we have?*

2   We usually use *many* and *much* in negative sentences and questions.
    *I don't go to **many** concerts.   He doesn't listen to **much** music.*
    *How **many** sandwiches do you want?   How **much** homework do you have?*

    In affirmative sentences, we normally use *a lot of* or *lots of*.
    *Chris has **lots of / a lot of** books.   We have **lots of / a lot of** homework.*

some and any

1   We use *some* and *any* with plural nouns and noncount nouns.
    ***some** apples   **some** food*   ***any** apples   **any** food*

2   We use *some* for an unspecific number or amount. We normally use *some* in affirmative sentences.
    *I bought **some apples** at the supermarket.   I'm going to buy **some food**.*

3   We normally use *any* in negative sentences and questions.
    *There weren't **any books** in the room.   Is there **any food** in the fridge?*

Unit 9

Comparative adjectives

1 When we want to compare two things, or two groups of things, we use a comparative form + *than*.

I'm **older than** my brother.   TVs are **more expensive than** radios.
Mexico is **bigger than** Costa Rica.   Your computer is **better than** mine.

2 With short adjectives, we normally add *er*.

old – older   *cheap – cheaper*   *small – smaller*

If the adjective ends in *e*, we add only *r*.

nice – nicer   *safe – safer*

If the adjective ends with consonant + *y*, we change the *y* to *i* and add *er*.

easy – easier   *early – earlier*   *happy – happier*

If the adjective ends in 1 vowel + 1 consonant, we double the final consonant and add *er*.

big – bigger   *sad – sadder*   *thin – thinner*

3 With longer adjectives (more than two syllables), we don't change the adjective. We put *more* in front of it.

expensive – more expensive
difficult – more difficult
interesting – more interesting

4 Some adjectives are irregular. They have a different comparative form.

good – better   *bad – worse*   *far – farther*

Superlative adjectives

1 When we compare something with two or more other things, we use a superlative form with *the*.

Steve is **the tallest** boy in our class.   This is **the most important** day of my life.
Brazil is **the biggest** country in South America.   Monday is **the worst** day of the week!

2 With short adjectives, we normally add *est*.

tall – the tallest   *old – the oldest*
short – the shortest   *clean – the cleanest*

Spelling rules for the *est* ending are the same as for the *er* ending in the comparative form.

nice – nicest   *safe – the safest*
easy – the easiest   *happy – the happiest*
big – the biggest   *thin – the thinnest*

3 With longer adjectives (more than two syllables), we don't change the adjective.
We put *the most* in front of it.

delicious – the most delicious
important – the most important
intelligent – the most intelligent

4 Some adjectives are irregular.

good – the best   *bad – the worst*   *far – the farthest*
I like Sundays, but I think Saturday is **the best** day of the week.
My team is terrible. It's **the worst** team in the world!

Unit 10

Present continuous for future arrangements

1 We can use the present continuous to talk about things that are planned or arranged for the future.

I'm **traveling** to Italy next week.   We're **having** a party on Saturday.   Alan **is meeting** Judy tomorrow.

2 Future time expressions are often used with the present continuous for arrangements.

tomorrow   *tomorrow night*   *next week*   *next Sunday evening*
the day after tomorrow   *the week after next*   *in three hours*

3 For information on the form of the present continuous, see the notes for Unit 4.

Unit 11

will/won't

1 We use *will* (*'ll*) and *won't* to make predictions about the future.

   *When I'm older, I'll **live** in France.*   *I **won't live** in England.*
   *I'm sure you'll **pass** the test tomorrow.*   *The questions **won't be** very difficult.*
   *In the future, people **will travel** to Mars.*   *But people **won't live** on Mars.*

2 *Will* is a modal (see also *must*, Unit 13 and *should*, Unit 15). We use *will/won't* + base form of the verb, and the form is the same for all subjects. We don't use any form of *do* in the negative.

   *You'll **pass** the test.*   *You **won't pass** the test.*
   *He'll **pass** the test.*   *He **won't pass** the test.*
   *Most students **will pass** the test.*   *Most students **won't pass** the test.*

3 Questions are formed with *will* + subject + base form of the verb. Again, we don't use any form of *do* in questions or short answers.

   ***Will** Sonia **go** to college?*   *Yes, she **will**. / No, she **won't**.*
   ***Will** your brothers **come** to the party?*   *Yes, they **will**. / No, they **won't**.*
   *When **will** the letter **arrive**?*

Unit 12

too + adjective

1 The adverb *too* + adjective has a negative meaning. When we use *too*, we mean "more than is good" or "more than I want."

   *I only have $300, and the TV costs $500. It's **too expensive**.*
   *It's only 5° today. I don't want to go out. It's **too cold**.*

2 Compare *too* with *very*, which doesn't have a negative meaning.

   *This computer costs $3,000. It's **very expensive**. But I have a lot of money, so for me it isn't **too expensive**.*

Adverbs

1 Adverbs usually go with verbs. They describe actions.

   *We <u>walked</u> home **slowly**.*   *The train <u>arrived</u> **late**.*
   *<u>Drive</u> **carefully**!*

   Some adverbs can also go with adjectives.

   *It was **bitterly** <u>cold</u> yesterday.*   *I get **extremely** <u>nervous</u> before my exam.*
   *They have an **incredibly** <u>large</u> house.*

2 A lot of adverbs are formed by adjective + *ly*.

   quiet – quietly   bad – badly   polite – politely

   If the adjective ends in *le*, we drop the *e* and add *y*.

   terrible – terribly   comfortable – comfortably

   If the adjective ends in consonant + *y*, we change the *y* to *i* and add *ly*.

   easy – easily   happy – happily   lucky – luckily

3 Some adverbs are irregular. They don't have an *ly* ending.

   *good – **well**   fast – **fast**   hard – **hard**   early – **early**   late – **late***
   *Our team played **well** on Saturday.*   *They worked **hard** all day.*
   *Susie can run **fast**.*

Unit 13

be going to: intentions

1 We use *be going to* to talk about things we intend to do in the future.
   I'm going to visit my grandfather next weekend.
   Marco is going to buy some new jeans tomorrow.

2 The form is the simple present of *be* + *going to* + base form of the verb.
   I'm going to stay at home on Sunday.   *I'm not going to play basketball.*
   She's going to do the dishes.   *She isn't going to spend much money.*

3 The question is formed with the simple present of *be* + subject + *going to* + base form of the verb.
   Are you going to watch the movie tonight?   *Yes, I am. / No, I'm not.*
   Is Paul going to meet you after school?   *Yes, he is. / No, he isn't.*
   Are your parents going to buy a car?   *Yes, they are. / No, they aren't.*
   When is she going to learn to drive?

be going to: predictions

We can also use **be going to** to make predictions based on things we know or can see.
Look at the clouds. It's going to rain soon.
Silvana didn't call her parents. They're going to be angry with her.

must/can't

1 *Must* is similar to *have to*. We use it to say that it is necessary or very important to do something.
   You must come home before 11 o'clock.
   I'm late. I must go!

2 We use *can't* to say that it is necessary or very important not to do something.
   You can't be late.
   I can't forget to go to the bank.

   Can't has a different meaning from *don't/doesn't have to*.
   You don't have to leave now. (= It isn't necessary for you to leave, although you can if you want to.)
   You can't leave now. (= Don't go. You must stay here!)

3 *Must* is a modal, like *will* (see Unit 11). We use *must* or *can't* + base form of the verb, and the form is the same for all subjects. We don't use any form of *do* in the negative.
   I must get up early tomorrow.   *I can't miss the train.*
   You must turn off your cell phone.   *You can't use it in the library.*

Unit 14

First conditional

1 In conditional sentences there are two clauses, an *if* clause and a result clause. We use the first conditional when it is possible or likely that the situation in the *if* clause will happen in the future.
   If I pass the test, my parents will be happy. (= It's possible that I'll pass, but I'm not sure.)
   If it doesn't rain, we'll go for a walk. (= Maybe it will rain, but I'm not sure.)

2 The *if* clause is formed with *If* + subject + simple present. The result clause is formed with subject + *will* + base form of the verb. There is a comma after the *if* clause.
   If he sees Martina, he'll tell her about the party.
   If we have time, we'll go shopping at the supermarket.
   If you don't start your homework soon, you won't finish it tonight.

3 We can change the order of the two clauses. In this case, there is no comma between the clauses.
   He'll tell Martina about the party if he sees her.
   We'll go shopping at the supermarket if we have time.

when and *if*

If indicates a possible situation. If we use *when* instead of *if*, it indicates that we are sure that the situation is going to happen.
If he sees Martina, he'll tell her about the party. (= Maybe he'll see her, maybe not.)
When he sees Martina, he'll tell her about the party. (= He's going to see her. This will definitely happen.)

Unit 15

should/shouldn't

1 When we want to say that something is a good idea (or is not a good idea), we can use *should* or *shouldn't*.

I **should work** this evening.	(I think this is a good idea for me.)
They **shouldn't buy** that computer.	(I think this is a bad idea for them.)
Should we **go** home now?	(Do you think this is a good idea for us?)

2 *Should* is another modal, like *will*, *must* and *can't*. We use *should/shouldn't* + base form of the verb, and the form is the same for all subjects. We don't use any form of *do* in the negative.

I **should lose** some weight.	I **shouldn't eat** this chocolate.
You **should come** to the game with us.	You **shouldn't stay** at home by yourself.

3 Questions are formed with *will* + subject + base form of the verb. Again, we don't use any form of *do* in questions or short answers.

Should we **wait** for Lisa?	Yes, we **should**. / No, we **shouldn't**.
Should I **tell** my parents?	Yes, you **should**. / No, you **shouldn't**.

What's it like?

1 We use a form of the question *What's it like?* if we want to hear a description or opinion of something/somebody. The answer to this question will often contain adjectives.

What's she **like**?	She's an interesting person, and she's very intelligent.
What are your neighbors **like**?	They're OK. They're polite, but they're not very friendly.

2 The question is formed with *What* + *be* + subject + *like*? The word *like* doesn't change. It's different from the verb *like*.

What's the weather **like** today?	**What was** the movie **like** last night?
What are those desserts **like**?	Did you meet Helen's cousins? **What were** they **like**?

Unit 16

Present perfect + *ever/never*

1 We often use the present perfect to talk about things from the beginning of our life until now.

John **has traveled** to a lot of different countries. (= from when he was born until now)
I **haven't met** your brother. (= at any time in my life, from when I was born until now)

2 When we use the present perfect with this meaning, we often use *ever* (= at any time in someone's life) in questions, and *never* (= not ever) in sentences.

Have you **ever eaten** seafood?	I've **never been** interested in music.
Has Steve **ever won** a prize in a competition?	She's **never tried** to cook.

3 The present perfect is formed with the present tense of *have* + past participle of the main verb.

For regular verbs, the past participle has the same *ed* ending as the simple past.
Irregular verbs have different past participles.

Regular verbs	Irregular verbs
We've stay**ed** in Athens three times.	We've **been** there three times.
Julia hasn't us**ed** a computer.	She hasn't **written** any emails.
Have they ever climb**ed** a mountain?	Have they ever **flown** on a plane?

For the past participles of irregular verbs, see the list on page 122 of the Student's Book.

4 Present perfect questions are formed with *have/has* + subject + past participle.

Have you ever **seen** a snake?	Yes, I **have**. / No, I **haven't**.
Has he ever **had** a job?	Yes, he **has**. / No, he **hasn't**.

Notes

Notes

Notes

Notes

Notes

Notes

Notes

Notes

Notes

Notes

Notes

Notes

Notes

Notes

Notes

Thanks and acknowledgments

The authors would like to thank a number of people whose support has proved invaluable during the planning, writing and production process of *American English in Mind*.

First of all we would like to thank the numerous teachers and students in many countries of the world who have used the first edition of *English in Mind*. Their enthusiasm for the course, and the detailed feedback and valuable suggestions we got from many of them were an important source of inspiration and guidance for us in developing the concept and in the creation of *American English in Mind*.

In particular, the authors and publishers would like to thank the following teachers who gave up their valuable time for classroom observations, interviews and focus groups:

Brazil

Warren Cragg (ASAP Idiomas); Angela Pinheiro da Cruz (Colégio São Bento; Carpe Diem); Ana Paula Vedovato Maestrello (Colégio Beatíssima Virgem Maria); Natália Mantovanelli Fontana (Lord's Idiomas); Renata Condi de Souza (Colégio Rio Branco, Higienópolis Branch); Alexandra Arruda Cardoso de Almeida (Colégio Guilherme Dumont Villares / Colégio Emilie de Villeneuve); Gisele Siqueira (Speak Up); Ana Karina Giusti Mantovani (Idéia Escolas de Línguas); Maria Virgínia G. B. de Lebron (UFTM / private lessons); Marina Piccinato (Speak Up); Patrícia Nero (Cultura Inglesa / Vila Mariana); Graziela Barroso (Associação Alumni); Francisco Carlos Peinado (Wording); Maria Lúcia Sciamarelli (Colégio Divina Providencia / Jundiaí); Deborah Hallal Jorge (Nice Time Language Center); Lilian Itzicovitch Leventhal (Colégio I. L. Peretz); Dulcinéia Ferreira (One Way Línguas); and Priscila Prieto and Carolina Cruz Marques (Seven Idiomas).

Colombia

Luz Amparo Chacón (Gimnasio Los Monjes); Mayra Barrera; Diana de la Pava (Colegio de la Presentación Las Ferias); Edgar Ardila (Col. Mayor José Celestino Mutis); Sandra Cavanzo B. (Liceo Campo David); Claudia Susana Contreras and Luz Marína Zuluaga (Colegio Anglo Americano); Celina Roldán and Angel Torres (Liceo Cervantes del Norte); Nelson Navarro; Maritza Ruiz Martín; Francisco Mejía, and Adriana Villalba (Colegio Calasanz).

Ecuador

Paul Viteri (Colegio Andino, Quito); William E. Yugsan (Golden Gate Academy – Quito); Irene Costales (Unidad Educativa Cardinal Spellman Femenino); Vinicio Sanchez and Sandra Milena Rodríguez (Colegio Santo Domingo de Guzmán); Sandra Rigazio and María Elena Moncayo (Unidad Educativa Tomás Moro, Quito); Jenny Alexandra Jara Recalde and Estanislao Javier Pauta (COTAC, Quito); Verónica Landázuri and Marisela Madrid (Unidad Educativa "San Francisco de Sales"); Oswaldo Gonzalez and Monica Tamayo (Angel Polibio Chaves School, Quito); Rosario Llerena and Tania Abad (Isaac Newton, Quito); María Fernanda Mármol Mazzini and Luis Armijos (Unidad Educativa Letort, Quito); and Diego Bastidas and Gonzalo Estrella (Colegio Gonzaga, Quito).

Mexico

Connie Alvarez (Colegio Makarenko); Julieta Zelinski (Colegio Williams); Patricia Avila (Liceo Ibero Mexicano); Patricia Cervantes de Brofft (Colegio Frances del Pedregal); Alicia Sotelo (Colegio Simon Bolivar); Patricia Lopez (Instituto Mexico, A.C.); Maria Eugenia Fernandez Castro (Instituto Oriente Arboledas); Lilian Ariadne Lozano Bustos (Universidad Tecmilenio); Maria del Consuelo Contreras Estrada (Liceo Albert Einstein); Alfonso Rene Pelayo Garcia (Colegio Tomas Alva Edison); Ana Pilar Gonzalez (Instituto Felix de Jesus Rougier); and Blanca Kreutter (Instituto Simon Bolivar).

Our heartfelt thanks go to the *American English in Mind* team for their cooperative spirit, their many excellent suggestions and their dedication, which have been characteristic of the entire editorial process: Paul Phillips, Amy E. Hawley, Kelley Perrella, Eric Zuarino, Pam Harris, Kate Powers, Brigit Dermott, Kate Spencer, Heather McCarron, Keaton Babb, Roderick Gammon, Hugo Loyola, Howard Siegelman, Colleen Schumacher, Margaret Brooks, Kathryn O'Dell, Genevieve Kocienda, Lisa Hutchins, and Lynne Robertson.

We would also like to thank the teams of educational consultants, representatives and managers working for Cambridge University Press in various countries around the world. Space does not allow us to mention them all by name here, but we are extremely grateful for their support and their commitment.

In Student's Book 2, thanks go to David Crystal for the interview in Unit 9, and to Jon Turner for giving us the idea of using the story of Ulises de la Cruz in Unit 15.

Thanks to the team at Pentacor for giving the book its design; the staff at Full House Productions for the audio recordings; and Lightning Pictures and Mannic Media for the video.

Last but not least, we would like to thank our partners, Mares and Adriana, for their support.

The publishers are grateful to the following illustrators:

Kel Dyson c/o The Bright Agency, Dylan Gibson, Ivan Gillett c/o NB Illustration, Graham Kennedy, Laura Martinez c/o Sylvie Poggio Artists Agency, Paul McCaffrey c/o Sylvie Poggio Artists Agency, Red Jelly, Mark Watkinson c/o Illustration.

The publishers are grateful to the following for permission to reproduce photographic material:

Key: l = left, c = center, r = right, t = top, b = bottom, u = upper, lo = lower, f = far.

Alamy/©Associated Sports Photography p 89, /©Pictorial Press Ltd p 77, Corbis/©Bettmann p 42 (D), /©Reed Kaestner p 69, /©James Marshall p 44, /©Robert Michael p 48 (br), /©Michael Ochs Archives p 26 (br); Diabolik@Astorina Srl www.diabolik.it p 30; Education Photos/ John Walmsley p 88; Getty Images/Hulton Archive/ General Photographic Agency p 42 (B), /David McNew p 26 (tl), /Photographer's Choice/ Peet Simard p 18 (tl), /Stock4B/Arne Pastoor p 20, /Taxi/ Ting Hoo p 18 (c), /Taxi/Erin Patrice O'Brien p 18 (bl); iStockphoto.com/BlackJack3D p 22 (1), /emrah oztas p 22 (3), /track5 p 18 (br); Masterfile/David Schmidt p 48 (tr); Photolibrary.com/ Comstock/Creatas p 48 (l), /Images Source p 18 (tc), /Ingram Publishing p 53, / Rex Features p 42 (C), /James McCauley p 42 (E); Shutterstock Images/LubaShi p 22 (2 /nart p 22 (7), / stocksnapp p 22 (6), /terekhov igor p 22 (8).

Alamy/PhotoAlto p4; AP Photo/Tom Gannam p6 ©; AP Photo/ Tom Gannam p6 (inset); Getty Images/Black 100 /Allsport Concepts/ p8; Alamy/image100 p11; iStockphoto.com/ Laurent Davoust p12 (tl); iStockphoto.com/Don Bayley p12 (tc); iStockphoto.com/Rena Schild p12 (tr); Getty Images/Ragnar p12 (cl); iStockphoto.com/williv p12 (cr); Getty Images/Jochen Sand /Photodisc p21; iStockphoto.com/blaneyphoto p22 (4); Shutterstock/Olga Sapegina p22 (5); Getty Images/Popperfoto p 42 (tr); Getty Images/Gary Cralle /The Image Bank p52; Cutcaster/Yuri Arcurs p90

The publishers are grateful to the following for their assistance with commissioned photographs: Mannic Media